_Acknowl..._

CU00890708

During 2007 my wife Bev (Mrs J as she is known on Twitter), was diagnosed with Secondary Progressive Multiple Sclerosis. Quickly the condition got a hold and it became apparent that Bev's cooking days were coming to an end. I had always enjoyed her cooking, we ate everything from fresh food and her meals were simply tasty and beautiful. We had 2 short weeks of frozen meals that I would put in the oven. That was enough; the time had come for Bev to now teach me to cook. I used to get Bev to sit on a chair in the kitchen and teach me every weekend. The meals I cooked were then frozen and were ready for me to cook off when I came home from the office. Within months, Bev told me I was on my own and I had mastered the basics. What a feeling that was! Now fast forward to this book and I feel it's remarkable what I have achieved.

Bev (Mrs J), without you and the patience you had with me this book wouldn't be here in print now. For that reason alone this book is dedicated to you. I thank you from the bottom of my heart and will always love you. Keep believing and smiling, between us we can do this x

Thank you to everyone who has contributed a recipe to #cookerysos, I asked and you answered.

Twitter Chefs/Twitter Friends/Facebook/Instagram, there are so many of you to thank. It would take another book just to make sure I got all the names entered. Seriously, I thank each and every one of you who picked up on the #icecoldchef. Your constant support and tips always inspired me further, I'll never forget the words you all told me "keep food simple". This book show's I have stuck to those principles and without your support this book wouldn't be here either.

_1_

I would also like to thank Sue at Netherton Foundry, Natalie from Ioshen Knives, Martyn from Wavygrain Boards and David & Sue from Embroidery Unit. Your products have been invaluable in the growth of the #icecoldchef.

Work Colleagues, I must have driven you mad over the years constantly talking about different recipes. I thank all of you for the support you have given me. There are too many to mention by name but once again I thank All of you.

Kirsten, I was struggling to get the book completed due to just not having enough time. You stepped in and started typing countless recipes I was emailing to you. Your help in this was exceptional and gave me that push to get the book completed, Thank you.

Howard & Air Products, I was racking my brains to see how I could raise the monies to send the book to print. I sent a tweet out and the rest is history, you stepped in with the Air Products Company and paid for the books to be printed. A massive Thank you.

Finally, thank you to Ian and Nat from Kissed Off Publishers. Your faith and belief in me from the start is appreciated. From a man that began his working life as a bricklayer to now an author is truly remarkable.

Enjoy #cookerysos and keep it simple.

John Joyce - Ice Cold Chef

Follow the #icecoldchef on Facebook/Twitter/Instagram

For more great recipes and cookery tips visit:
www.icecoldchef.co.uk

2

Foreword

This book was the idea of my husband John and was produced in an effort to help others who might find themselves in the same and similar situations to ours. It came about originally out of necessity but has since become something that is a lot more meaningful to us. All proceeds will be donated to charity.

John is not, nor has he ever professed to be, a qualified chef. He is an ordinary man, who works and also happens to care for me, his wife.

Eight years ago, we were your "average" couple, with one daughter, Louise who were living life as we wanted, going along nicely. John was a brick layer, I worked for the DWP and our daughter had just moved into her first house. John had decided on a career change as he didn't want to work away from home any longer. He applied for and secured a job with Blackpool Council. It was a big change adapting to the office world, but as with everything he does, John put in one hundred per cent and really took to it.

Unfortunately, at the same time, I began to have strange symptoms and feelings in my legs that resulted in me being referred to a neurologist and eventually being diagnosed with Secondary Progressive Multiple Sclerosis.

I enjoyed and had always done all the cooking at home. However my progression into MS was so fast that it soon became apparent that I could no longer continue to do this. We tried various processed foods, but within a couple of weeks knew that this wasn't for us. John asked me to teach him to cook. I taught him the basics but as ever John took to it and decided to take things a lot further. He started to talk about cooking on social media and was soon receiving encouragement, ideas and recipes from chefs and other amateur cooks from all over the world. This support gave John the idea to put his and their recipes into a book, firstly to show anyone they can cook if they really want to and secondly to raise money for charity.

John was invited to cook live at the MS convention in Manchester and at various other food festivals. This has provided us with an avenue to go out, to meet people and to become involved in different events. We are able to support several local charities through John's cooking, raising funds by selling his food.

Earlier this year John was nominated for, by the Blackpool Carers Trust and won the Adult Carer of the year award for 2014. This has led to John being asked to teach young carers to cook, which he is honoured to do.

We try not to ask "why" MS came into our lives but we do know you do not have to lie down and give up. There is still a life to live, just a different one than you might have planned.

I can honestly say, we are happy and receive a lot of enjoyment and fulfilment knowing that we may inspire and help others in their hour of need.

Bev Joyce, July 2015

Contents

How to Use This Book

This book has been created to ease you into creating tasty, affordable and simple meals as you start out on your cookery journey.

We have taken the time to test each recipe that has been kindly donated, as well as suggesting alternative ingredients where allergy, medical reasons or personal taste dictates.

Calorie counts are only a loose guide along with servings as these will obviously vary on portion sizes and appetites. These reflect calories per serving and not per recipe.

These recipes are intended as a guide, we want you to continue to experiment with flavours until you find your feet as a cook. Even while we produced this book we've continued to experiment with the recipes and see the helpful hints section at the end for all questions you may have.

We've also included conversion tables at the end of the book for those using gas/fan ovens and other cooking appliances.

As always, please ensure food is cooked thoroughly before serving - every appliance has its own unique habits and times may vary between ovens and appliances.

Cooking times and temperatures are based on a conventional oven.

Mexican Tacos

Contributed by John Joyce

Ingredients

- 250g mince beef
- 1 onion
- 1 box tacos
- 1 small tin kidney beans
- 1 tin tomatoes

- Taco seasoning mix or your own spices
- Chilli flakes – if you want it hot/ spicy
- Bag mixed salad of your choice
- Any grated cheese if you wish

Method

1. Preheat the oven to 180°C.

2. Add a splash of oil to pan & brown off the mince.

3. Add the onion & season mix & chilli flakes, if using.

4. Add the tin of tomatoes & on a medium heat let the pan begin to bubble.

5. Turn the heat down again and let the liquid reduce. This could take 10 mins or more - the aim is to have a drier mix to add to the tacos.

6. Follow the instructions for the tacos and stand them end down on a tray. Bake for 2-3 mins.

7. Once ready, fill your tacos with the mince beef mix - by now it should be full of flavour and rich in colour.

Add salad leaves of your choice on top and grated cheese if you wish.
ENJOY.

Serves: 4

Calories: 391
Allergens: Taco Mix can contain Cloves
Alternatives: Fajita Mix on p. 71

Ciabatta Pizza

Contributed by John Joyce

Ingredients

- 1 ciabatta bread
- Any leftover cheese
- Packet of pepperoni
- 2-3 tomatoes
- 1 tbsp tomato puree
- Fresh basil
- 1 tbsp olive oil

Method

1. Preheat the oven to 200°C.

2. Cut the ciabatta in half lengthways.

3. Spread the tomato puree over the tops of the ciabatta.

4. Crumble or grate the cheese over the puree.

5. Slice the tomatoes & add on top of the cheese.

6. Add slices of pepperoni to suit your taste.

7. Drizzle over the olive oil.

8. Finally add the chopped basil.

9. Bake in the oven for 10-12 mins.

Makes: 4

Calories: 483
Allergens: Gluten
Alternatives:
Parma ham,
mushrooms

Enjoy in front of a great movie! Finger food at its best. We swapped the pepperoni for parma ham which brings this down to 196 calories per slice.

Cider Rarebit

Contributed by Alan Paton

Ingredients

- 4oz butter
- 1oz plain flour
- ½ lb grated mature cheddar (Suffolk gold or similar)
- ½ pint Aspall's Cider
- 1 tsp paprika
- 1 tsp mustard powder or 2 tsp English mustard
- 4 yolks beaten

Method

1. Melt butter, add flour and cook for 4-5 mins.

2. Add cider in stages mixing well with spatula or wooden spoon.

3. Cook over medium heat for 12-15 mins stirring regularly.

4. Mix paprika, mustard and egg yolk to a paste, beat into cider mix.

5. Cool and refrigerate until needed.

6. To serve, lightly warm up and serve in dipping bowl or spread on to Cheese Biscuits *p.47* and glaze under the grill, allow to cool and set before devouring. Perfect as an occasional treat.

Calorie calculation is based only on this element. If you are following a calorie controlled diet, please add to this figure whatever you serve this with.

Serves: 4

Calories: 412
Allergens: Dairy
Alternatives:
Dairy free cheese

Burger Meal

Contributed by John Joyce

Ingredients

- 2 beef burgers (use your local butcher where you can)
- 1 onion chopped
- 1 garlic clove crushed
- 12-14 cherry tomatoes (or any tomato if you don't have them)
- 12-14 button mushrooms
- 2 slices of blue cheese
- 30-40ml water
- 2 bread rolls
- 1 tsp tomato puree
- Salt & pepper
- 3-4 tbsp olive oil

Method

1. Heat a frying pan over a medium heat and add 2 tbsp of olive oil.

2. Add the 2 burgers and fry on both side to add colour, around 3 mins each side.

3. Remove the burgers when you are happy with the colour. Place on a plate to one side.

4. Add the onions, garlic and mushrooms and finally the tomatoes.

5. I add a splash of water to the pan and add the tomato puree.

6. Now place the burgers back in the pan and cover with the juices. Heat the burgers through again, they won't take long.

Makes: 2

Calories: 779
Allergens: Gluten

Serve on a bread roll and add a slice of blue cheese. Put the top on and enjoy

Italian Gnocchi

Contributed by John Joyce

Ingredients

- 1 tbsp olive oil
- 1 packet shop-bought gnocchi
- ½ lb mince beef
- 2 or 3 crushed garlic cloves
- Italian herb mix – any will do
- 1 tin tomatoes
- 2-3 onions, chopped
- 6-8 mushrooms, sliced
- Salt & pepper
- Grated parmesan or any cheese you have

Method

1. Add the oil to a large pan over a medium heat. Then place your mince in when the oil has warmed up. Brown your mince and remove when ready; put to one side.

2. Add the onions, mushrooms and garlic and cook until all has softened and taken on the flavours. Now place the mince back into the pan and stir together. Add the tomatoes from the tin and fill the empty tin with water from the tap. Add this to the pan and reduce by half over a medium heat. Add salt & pepper to taste.

3. Finally add the gnocchi and cook through – 5 mins should suffice but check one to make sure.

4. Plate up and add your grated cheese/parmesan.

Enjoy!

Serves: 4

Calories: 543
Allergens:
Egg, Gluten
Alternatives:
"Free from"
Gnocchi

Frittata

Contributed by John Joyce

Ingredients

- 2 tbsp olive oil
- 400g leftover cooked new potatoes, sliced
- 4 eggs, beaten
- 4 spring onions, finely sliced
- 1 bunch dill, roughly chopped
- 35g cheddar, grated

Method

1. In a frying pan, heat the oil over a medium heat.

2. Add potatoes, then fry until beginning to crisp, around 10 mins.

3. Whisk together eggs, spring onions, dill in a large bowl.

4. Turn the grill on.

5. Add the eggs into frying pan, mix quickly and lower the heat, then sprinkle over cheese.

6. After about 7-8 mins, once the top side has almost set.

7. Put the pan under the grill for 2-3 mins or until firm and golden.

8. Then slide out of the pan gently.

Serves: 8

Calories: 108
Allergens:
Egg, Dairy
Alternatives:
Dairy free cheese

Serve immediately with red or brown sauce.

Prosciutto, Mushrooms & Tomatoes

Contributed by John Joyce

Ingredients

- 1 pack of prosciutto
- 12-14 button mushrooms
- 10-12 cherry tomatoes
- 2 tbsp olive oil
- 1 tbsp balsamic vinegar
- 1 tsp dried basil
- Salt & pepper
- Uncut bread sliced or bread rolls

Method

1. Preheat the oven to 200°C.

2. Place the prosciutto on a non-stick oven tray and place in the oven.

3. Heat a frying pan over a medium heat and add the olive oil.

4. Add the mushrooms to the pan.

5. Put a small slit into the tomatoes and add to the pan, the slit will stop them popping and keep the shape.

6. Add the balsamic vinegar, basil and salt & pepper.

7. Check the prosciutto in the oven, 10 mins and it should be ready.

8. Now serve the prosciutto on the your chosen bread, add the mushrooms & tomatoes and dress with red or brown sauce.

Nothing beats the weekend breakfast, we tend to have this as brunch, just simple ingredients.

Serves: 3

Calories: 391
Allergens: Gluten
Alternatives:
Pitta bread or
"free from"
bread rolls

13

Burger Baguettes

Contributed by Kirsten Huesch

Ingredients

- 1 pack "bake at home" baguettes (usually 2 in a pack, 200g in total)
- 400g mince beef (any other mince will also work although I haven't tried vegetarian mince with this)
- 1 medium onion, cut into small pieces
- 1 egg
- Salt & pepper
- Breadcrumbs
- Few gherkins, sliced
- Tomato ketchup
- Few slices of cheese (enough to cover each piece of baguette)

Method

1. Preheat the oven to 220°C .

2. In a bowl, combine the raw mince with the egg, onion, salt and pepper and breadcrumbs to form the burger "mix".

3. Cut the baguettes in half and slice horizontally.

4. Divide the burger mix evenly onto each piece of baguette, top with gherkins, then ketchup and finish off with cheese.

5. Pop the burger baguettes in the hot oven and bake for 15 mins.

Makes: 4

Calories: 469
Allergens:
Gluten, Egg
Alternatives:
Different minced
meat

Liver & Bacon

Contributed by John Joyce

Ingredients

- 8 rashers streaky bacon
- 2 tbsp seasoned flour (salt & pepper)
- 800g liver, sliced
- 1 tbsp oil
- 1 thick sliced onion
- 600ml stock
- 1 tbsp dried sage
- 2-3 tbsp olive oil

Method

1. Add the sage to the seasoned flour. Now add the sliced liver and give it a good coating.

2. Fry your bacon until as crispy as you like it over a medium heat. Remove from the pan when your bacon is ready.

3. Add the remainder of the oil to the pan. Shake the excess flour from the liver and fry for a couple of mins both sides.

4. Add the onion and fry until softened. Stir in the stock and let it bubble away for around 5 mins.

5. Add your liver back to the pan and cook for around 5 mins.

Serve with mashed potatoes

Serves: 4

Calories: 553
Allergens: None
Alternatives:
Parma ham

Filled Focaccia Rolls

Contributed by Sarah Bailey

Ingredients

- 12 oz strong white bread flour
- 1 rounded tsp fast action dried yeast
- 2 tbsp oil – olive or rapeseed are ideal
- 7½ fl oz warm water

- 2 rashers bacon, cooked and chopped
- 2 oz button mushrooms, chopped
- 1 large tomato, cut into six slices, or 6 pieces sundried tomato

Method

1. Mix the flour, yeast and salt in a large bowl, stir in the oil.

2. Add the water and mix to a dough, turn out onto a work surface and knead until smooth and elastic. Cover, and leave in a warm place until doubled in size, approx. 1 hour.

3. Turn the dough out onto a lightly floured work surface and 'knock back'. Divide into 6 equal pieces and roll them out into rectangles 3 x 12".

4. With the short ends towards you, mark the strips into four squares. In your mind, number them 1st, 2nd, 3rd and 4th starting with the square nearest to you.

5. Place ⅙ of the bacon on the square nearest to you.

6. Lift the dough from the other end and fold the second square over the bacon on the first square so that it is covered, press the cut edges together to seal.

7. Place ⅙ of the mushrooms on the 2nd square and lift again so that the third square covers the mushroom, press the cut edges together to seal.

8. Place a piece of tomato on the 3rd square and fold the 4th square over it, press to seal all the cut edges. This folding process is carried out 'concertina style'.

9. Place the focaccia rolls onto a greased baking sheet and leave to rise in a warm place for approx. 1 hour.

10. Preheat the oven to 220°C.

11. Bake for 25-30 mins.

Best eaten warm.
Ideal for a Brunch Menu, we used parma ham for the bacon flavour without the calories!

Serves: 6

Calories: 326
Allergens: Gluten
Alternatives:
Parma ham

Posh Cheese on Toast

Contributed by John Joyce

Ingredients

- 6 bacon rashers grilled (I used some prosciutto I had left)
- Any tomatoes you may have left chopped
- 1 tbsp balsamic vinegar
- 2 tbsp olive oil
- 300g mature grated cheese
- 1 tsp English mustard
- 2-3 dashes Tabasco
- 1 tsp Worcestershire sauce
- Salt & pepper to taste
- 2 ciabatta breads sliced

Method

1. Heat a pan over a medium heat and add the oil, then add the bacon to the pan.

2. Cook through until crispy, then remove and add the tomatoes & balsamic vinegar.

3. Once the tomatoes are ready and coloured add the bacon back to the pan and remove from the heat.

4. Mix the mustard, tobacco and Worcestershire sauce together in a small bowl.

5. Turn the grill on. Place the ciabatta breads under top side down and crisp up.

6. Remove and turn over. Spoon over the mixture across the ciabatta breads. Cover with the grated cheese and place back under the grill.

Serves: 6

Calories: 441
Allergens: Gluten

Remove when ready and add the crispy bacon and tomatoes across the top of the cheesy ciabatta breads. Enjoy with a nice mug of tea!

My Special Muesli

Contributed by John Joyce

You will need:

- 6-8 mugs porridge oats
- Handful of sultanas
- Any other dried fruit you want to add
- Nuts & seeds
- 1 tbsp honey
- Milk
- Pyrex Bowl

Method

1. Cover the oats/fruit mix with milk & add the honey.

2. Give the mixture a good stir around to mix it all up.

3. If required add more milk.

4. Cover with cling wrap & place in the fridge overnight.

5. The mixture will soak up the milk & the oats become soft. The mixture will have thickened.

6. Loosen up with a little milk & serve. If you have any fresh fruit, top it off with this or anything else you wish.

This is a slow release breakfast but so tasty & fresh. It will keep you going until lunch! Enjoy.

Serves: 6

Calories: 234

My Bacon on Toast

Contributed by John Joyce

Ingredients

- 1 pack of parma ham, finely sliced
- Sliced mushrooms or chopped tomatoes. In fact, anything you want to add on the top of your toast
- A splash of olive oil in a pan

This is my favourite weekend breakfast. I like to use a Real Bread loaf that I have baked myself. You can however buy one from your supermarket. Instead of back bacon I like to use Parma Ham, I find it gives a real fried breakfast taste but without all the fats.

Method

1. Turn your grill on full so it's ready to bring this tasty meal together.

2. Add the sliced parma ham to the pan and slowly fry in the olive oil. All we want to do is lightly fry the ham. As soon as you see it changing colour and crisping up remove from the heat and add it to a dish to keep warm.

3. Place the dish at the bottom of your oven, the heat from the grill will keep the ham warm. You can cover the dish too with foil.

4. Add another splash of olive oil to the pan and add the sliced mushrooms or tomatoes the pan. Again fry these gently, we don't want anything burned. Just a gentle fry and allow the moisture to evaporate.

5. Once these are ready, remove and add to the dish in the oven. Now it's time to toast your bread to the way you like it.

6. When you are happy, spread with a little butter or your preferred choice. Now build up your breakfast, I tend to start with a drizzle of brown sauce, then my mushrooms or tomatoes and finally add my parma ham.

7. Believe me, this bacon on toast is just packed full of flavour and gives you the feeling of eating a fried breakfast without all those calories.

8. Enjoy with a mug of tea.

Serves: 6

Calories: 78
Allergens: Gluten
Alternatives: Add a scrambled egg for a truly stuffed sandwich

Poached Egg

Contributed by John Joyce

Ingredients

- Eggs
- Salt & pepper
- 1 tbsp white wine vinegar

Method

1. Fill a small pan just over one third full with cold water and bring it to the boil.

2. Add the vinegar and turn down to simmer.

3. Crack the eggs one at a time into a small bowl and gently tip into the simmering water.

4. Lightly poach for 3-4 mins.

5. Remove with a slotted spoon and drain on kitchen towels.

6. These are a great way to enjoy your egg, take your time and keep the pan on a low simmer.

Serves: 1

Calories: 90
Allergens:
Egg, Gluten

Enjoy with toast or even add them on top of a summer salad

22

Egg & Bacon Baskets

Contributed by John Joyce

Ingredients

- 12 slices bacon
- 12 fresh eggs
- ½ tsp salt
- ½ tsp pepper
- 2 tbsp olive oil

Method

1. Preheat oven 200°C.

2. In medium frying pan fry bacon to soft transparent stage.

3. Drain on paper towels.

4. Line each slice around the side of each muffin cup, you can overlap the bacon.

5. Break egg directly in the center of each muffin cup of a 12 cup muffin pan.

6. Slightly salt and pepper.

7. Cook 15-20 mins.

8. Watch for whites and yolks to begin to set.

9. Take out with small spatula on a serving plate.

10. Serve with fork and knife.

11. These are nice with toast or part of a Sunday breakfast, again you decide and enjoy

Serves: 6

Calories: 418
Allergens: Egg
Alternatives: Prosciutto

Granola

Contributed by Kirsten Huesch

Ingredients

- 150ml maple syrup
- 2 tbsp honey
- 1 tsp vanilla extract (optional) - or replace with cinnamon
- 300g rolled oats
- 50g sunflower seeds
- 4 tbsp sesame seeds
- 50g pumpkin seeds
- 100g flaked almonds
- 100g dried berries (find them in the baking aisle)
- 50g coconuts flakes or desiccated coconut (optional)

Method

1. Heat oven to 150°C. Mix the maple syrup, honey and vanilla (or cinnamon if using) in a large bowl. Tip in all the remaining ingredients, except the dried fruit and coconut, and mix well.

2. Tip the granola onto two baking sheets and spread evenly.

3. Bake for 15 mins, then mix in the coconut and dried fruit, and bake for 10-15 mins more.

4. Remove and scrape onto a flat tray to cool.

5. Serve with cold milk or yogurt.

Serves: 12

Calories: 304

The granola can be stored in an airtight container for up to a month. Try mixing fruits and seeds for different flavour combinations.

French Toast Quiche

Contributed by Kirsten Huesch

Ingredients

- 6 slices of buttered bread
- 500ml milk
- 3 eggs
- 150g grated cheese (cheddar or similar)
- Salt & pepper
- 1 stock cube
- Some ham or bacon, cut into strips
- 2 tomatoes, sliced

Method

1. Preheat the oven to 160°C (fan oven).

2. Butter the bread and place, buttered side down, into an ovenproof dish/casserole.

3. Mix the eggs with the milk and crumble in the stock cube; pour the mix over the bread.

4. Top with cheese, then ham or bacon strips and tomato slices.

5. Bake in the oven on the middle shelf for around 30-40 mins (this depends a little on your oven - just check after half an hour if the egg mix is cooked).

6. Serve hot with a side salad.

Why not add a little feta cheese and some basil and oregano for a Mediterranean touch?
Or leave out the ham/bacon to make it vegetarian? Simply use what you have to hand & love eating

Serves: 3-4

Calories: 370
Allergens: Egg

Soda Bread

Contributed by John Joyce

Ingredients

- 170g self-raising wholemeal flour
- 170g plain flour
- ½ tsp salt
- ½ tsp bicarbonate of soda
- 290ml buttermilk

Method

1. Preheat the oven to 200°C.

2. Place the flours, salt and bicarbonate of soda into a large mixing bowl and mix together.

3. Make a small well in the centre and pour in the buttermilk.

4. Mix quickly together with a large fork to form a soft dough.

5. The dough should not be too dry or sticky, if required add a touch of milk or little flour.

6. Place the dough onto a lightly floured surface and knead briefly (don't overwork it).

7. Shape into a round and flatten the dough slightly before placing on a lightly floured baking tray.

8. Now cut a cross on the top and bake for about 30 mins or until the loaf sounds hollow.

9. Remove and allow to cool on a rack.

10. Serve with butter and a nice cup of tea.

Serves: 4-6

Calories: 215
Allergens: Gluten

26

Parmesan Crisps

Contributed by John Joyce

Ingredients

- 1 large mug of grated fresh Parmesan cheese
- Freshly ground black pepper (to taste)
- Baking sheet or parchment paper

Method

1. Preheat oven to 200°C.

2. Line a large baking sheet with parchment paper.

3. Use a spoon to add the cheese on the baking sheet at 2" apart.

4. Spread each mound to a 2" diameter. Sprinkle mounds with pepper.

5. Bake for 6-8 mins or until crisp and golden.

6. Cool completely on baking sheet.

7. Remove from baking sheet using a thin spatula.

Makes: 9
Calories: 10

27

Cheese & Tomato Tart

Contributed by John Joyce

Ingredients

- 1 packet shop bought puff pastry
- 3 tomatoes sliced
- 1 clove garlic crushed
- 1 pack feta cheese
- 1 tbsp dried basil
- 2-3 tbsp tomato puree
- Salt & pepper
- Flour for dusting

Method

1. Preheat 200°C and line a baking tray with baking paper.

2. Roll out the pastry.

3. Cut the pastry into 4 rectangles.

4. Now score a rectangle about 1" in from the pastry edge.

5. Spread the inner rectangle with tomato purée.

6. Lay slices of tomato and feta on top of the purée.

7. Sprinkle the basil over the tomatoes.

8. Sprinkle the feta with pepper.

9. Put the tarts on the baking tray.

10. Bake for about 20 mins until pastry is golden and risen.

Serves: 16

Calories: 45
Allergens:
Egg, dairy

Enjoy on their own or with a fresh salad. Try other fillings to vary the flavours!

Organic Onion Soup

Contributed by James Richards

Ingredients

- 3 large onions
- 3 cloves garlic
- 5 potatoes
- ½ pint of chicken stock
- 4 tsp Bisto
- Salt & pepper to taste

Method

1. Peel onions and cut in half and place in pan of water and bring to boil. As soon water is boiling, turn down to lowest temperature. Once onions are soft, take them out of pan and let them cool for a while.

2. Peel potatoes and cut into small pieces and place in pan of water and bring to the boil. As soon as the water is boiling, turn down to lowest temperature. As soon as they become soft, stop cooking and empty water and mash potatoes some unsalted butter and a little semi-skimmed milk.

3. Now blend or mash onions and as you do, add a little of the retained water to onions (from pan you cooked onions in) until onions become a stiff substance.

4. Next add onion mix to potatoes and stir together.

5. With the garlic, peel outer skin, then preferably crush or chop finely and place in mix and stir thoroughly.

6. Heat up chicken stock in a pan, then add Bisto granules. That's my lazy way of making the gravy, though you could make from scratch, up to you!. Next pour stock into jug and stir well. Now add stock gravy to onion mix and stir. Simmer for approximately 10-15 mins and add organic salt and pepper just before cooking is finished.

Pea and Mint Soup

Contributed by John Joyce

Ingredients

- 320g petit pois
- 150g diced onions
- 180g potatoes
- 20g butter
- 4g mint
- Salt & pepper

Method

1. Sweat off the diced onions in butter until soft.

2. Dice the potatoes, add to the onions and cover with water and bring to the simmer.

3. When the potatoes are nearly cooked then add the petit pois and the mint.

4. Take off the heat and empty into a blender and blend until smooth.

5. Alternatively, remove from the heat and use a hand blender and again, blend till smooth.

6. Add salt & pepper to your taste and serve.

Serves: 3-4

Calories: 122

30

Pea and Ham Soup

Contributed by John Joyce

Ingredients

- 1 large ham hock
- 6 large chopped carrots
- 4 sliced leeks
- 1 large onion finely chopped
- Large bag frozen mushy peas
- 1 herb pot
- Pepper

Method

1. I tend to remove the rind/skin before adding the ham hock to the pan.

2. Into a large pan add the ham hock, cover with water and start bringing it to the boil. As you chop your veg, add to the pan and bring it to the boil.

3. Once the pan has reached boiling point reduce, add the herb pot, pepper and simmer for a couple of hours.

4. After a couple of hours your ham hock should be done. Remove the ham hock ready to be shredded. Add your peas and bring the pan back up to the boil.

5. Meanwhile, shred the ham hock, I use 2 forks and pull the ham apart. Add the shredded ham back to the pan and bring it back up to the boil.

6. When the pan is boiling, reduce and simmer for an hour. Taste for flavour and if required top up with boiling water.

The mushy peas will thicken this soup very quickly, I tend to get this ready the night before we will eat it. Mine is in the pan inside the fridge for tonight's tea. Enjoy with a roll or dumplings!

Serves: 3-4

Calories: 324

Asian Broth

Contributed by Alan Paton

Ingredients

- 1kg cooked pork belly cut into dice
- 1.5 ltr pork stock OR you could use chicken or vegetable stock
- 1 bunch spring onions finely sliced
- 1 pack soba noodles 250g
- 50g peeled ginger diced
- 4 peeled garlic cloves, roughly chopped
- 4 sprigs coriander
- 2 limes zested and squeezed
- 200g oyster mushrooms, pulled into strips
- 100g shitake mushrooms sliced
- 1 tbsp peanut butter
- 600g shelled and de-veined tiger/king prawns sliced into pieces or halves
- 1 green chilli diced
- 2 red onion diced
- 1 bunch pak choi shredded
- 4 tbsp sesame oil
- 2 tbsp rice wine vinegar

Serves: 10

Calories: 430
Allergens: Seafood

Time to get your chopsticks out for this recipe, it will make 10 portions so amend as you see fit. The longer and slower you cook the pork belly make an altogether more pleasurable eat.

Method

1. Warm the sesame oil up in a large pan.

2. Add the red onion and half of the garlic and ginger, lightly brown.

3. Add the pork stock and bring to simmer.

4. Add the noodles (you can either leave whole or break down).

5. After 5 mins add the mushrooms and peanut butter.

6. The pork belly can either be sautéed for extra flavour separately and added or added now.

7. Once noodles are nearly cooked stir in all remaining ingredients, simmer for 5 mins.

8. Taste, season and serve.

Leek & Potato Soup

Contributed by John Joyce

Ingredients

- 4 leeks finely sliced
- 3 potatoes, chopped in small pieces
- 350ml veg stock
- Salt & pepper
- Parmesan cheese or whatever you make have in the fridge

Method

1. Add a splash of olive oil to your pan; then add the sliced leeks. Fry them off gently, this will give them a little colour and add flavour to the soup. They won't take long; then add your veg stock and the chopped potatoes.

2. Bring to the boil and gently simmer until all the veg in the soup has softened.

3. I allow the soup to cool and then add it to a food processor to blitz, you can use a potato masher if you wish.

4. Add the soup back to the pan, bring back up to the boil and simmer. Salt and pepper can be added to your taste.

5. A nice piece of Real Bread or bread roll makes this a tasty winter warmer.

Serves: 4

Calories: 186

Beef & Guinness Stew

Contributed by Nicky Vacca

Ingredients

- 25g butter
- 150g bacon lardons
- 300g shallots
- 1kg stewing beef
- 400g wild mushroom mixture
- 1 can Guinness
- 1 bouquet garni

Guinness and beef stew is a easy slow-cooked recipe that's great for a dinner party in the winter, just serve with lots of roast potatoes and green vegetables

Method

1. Preheat the oven to 160°C.

2. Put the butter in a frying pan over a medium heat. When the butter has melted add the bacon, followed by the shallots. Cook until golden brown and transfer to a large casserole.

3. Add the beef to the frying pan, season with salt & pepper and cook until browned all over. Transfer to the casserole. Add the mushrooms to the pan and cook for 2 mins. Season to taste, transfer to the casserole dish.

4. Return the frying pan to the heat and use a whisk to scrape off all the bits stuck to the bottom of the pan. Pour in the Guinness and continue to whisk for another minute to deglaze the pan. Pour the Guinness and pan juices over the beef and vegetables in the casserole. Add the bouquet garni, cover the casserole and cook in the oven for 2 hours.

5. When the beef is tender, check the seasoning, remove the bouquet garni and serve with roast potatoes.

Serves: 4

Calories: 1003

Creamy Chicken Soup

Contributed by Kirsten Huesch

Ingredients

- Little butter or oil
- 1 large carrot, cut into small cubes
- 1 leek, chopped
- 1 stick of celery, cut into small cubes
- 1 red bell pepper, cut into cubes
- 2 cloves of garlic, crushed
- A few chilli flakes (to taste)
- 2 chicken breasts, cubed
- 2 tbsp cornflour (to dust the chicken)
- 2 bacon rashers, cubed
- 250g cooked rice (good way to use up leftover rice or for extra speed, or why not use a packet of cooked microwave rice as a shortcut)
- 200ml evaporated milk - about half a can (I used a reduced fat version)
- 500ml water (you may need a little more to get the consistency you'd like)
- 1 chicken stock cube
- Salt & pepper to taste
- Good handful of chopped chives

Serves: 4

Calories: 580
Allergens: Celery
Alternatives:
Omit celery

This would also work well with added mushrooms or ham instead of the chicken.

Method

1. Heat the oil/butter in a large pan and add the chopped vegetables and garlic. Add the bacon and cook everything until the vegetables have softened.

2. Toss the chicken breast pieces in cornflour and add to the pan. Cook for a couple of mins, stirring frequently.

3. Now pour in the evaporated milk, sprinkle on the chilli flakes (if using) and crumble in the stock cube.

4. Add the cooked rice to the pan - the mixture will now be quite thick, so start adding water until you have the consistency you would like.

5. Heat through, add the chopped chives and adjust the seasoning.

Serve in bowls with chunks of bread on the side.

Tomato & Pepperoni Soup

Contributed by Helen McDonald

Ingredients

- 60g pepperoni slices, cut in half
- 1 onion, chopped
- 2 tbsp plain flour
- 2 x 400g chopped tomatoes
- 2 veg stock cubes
- Salt & pepper to taste
- Milk to dilute – optional
- Grated cheese to serve – optional

Method

1. Dry fry the pepperoni in a large pan/stock pot over a low heat. When the oil starts to come out of the pepperoni add the onion and continue to fry until soft.

2. Stir in the flour for 1-2 mins to make a roux which will help to thicken the soup later without the need for cornflour.

3. Next add the tomatoes and stock cubes, cover and simmer for 15 mins.

4. Blend with a hand blender and add salt & pepper to taste.

5. At this stage if the soup is too thick and rich, add milk and reheat being careful not to burn the milk.

Serve topped with grated cheese!

Serves: 2

Calories: 468

HINT - you can vary the quantity of pepperoni according to taste or use chorizo instead. Most supermarkets sell a pack of pepperoni for £1 and under so this can be a very economical meal.

38

Minestrone Soup

Contributed by John Joyce

Ingredients

- 1 finely chopped onion
- 3 finely chopped garlic cloves
- 400g of any veg you have chopped (I used celery, carrots, potatoes)
- Tin of chopped tomatoes
- Tin of borlotti beans or any beans of your choice
- 2 tsp of tomato puree
- ½ litre vegetable stock (homemade or a cube)
- 160g pasta, use whatever you have
- A little grated cheese to serve with

Method

1. Sauté the onion and garlic until soft but not coloured

2. Add in your chopped vegetables

3. Add the tomatoes, the beans and tomato puree

4. Stir well and add in the stock

5. Cook until the vegetables are just tender

6. Add in the pasta and cook for another 10 mins

7. Serve with the grated cheese sprinkled on top along with some crusty bread, even better use some of your real Bread

Serves: 2

Calories: 550
Allergens: Celery
Alternatives:
Try using other veg

Chicken & Coconut Thai Soup

Contributed by Gillian Thewlis

Ingredients

- 2 chicken breasts - chopped into pieces
- 1 spanish onion - roughly chopped
- 1-2 red chillies - sliced lengthways (top & tailed, deseeded)
- 1 large tsp lemongrass paste (buy in a jar from supermarket), or fresh lemongrass
- ½ piece grated ginger, or use ginger paste (buy in a jar from supermarket)
- 2 cloves garlic, crushed
- 3 spring onions, sliced lengthways
- 6 small button mushrooms
- 3 small cherry tomatoes
- 1 tin coconut milk
- 'Frylight' oil, or olive oil

Method

1. Add oil in pan.
2. Gently fry the chopped onion.
3. Add chopped chicken, gently brown.
4. Add chilli, garlic, lemongrass, ginger and gently fry.
5. When chicken cooked, add garlic, spring onions, mushroom, cherry tomatoes and coconut milk. Gently heat through, until mushrooms and tomatoes are cooked.
6. Then serve in deep bowls, garnished on top with fresh coriander.

Serves: 5

Calories: 429

Alternatively you can serve this as a curry with basmati rice, or fine egg noodles.

40

Chicken Broth

Contributed by Garmon Owen

Ingredients

- Use the leftover carcass of a chicken after your Sunday dinner.
- 3-4 potatoes
- 2 onions
- 1-2 cups frozen peas or sweetcorn
- Salt & pepper

Method

1. Place the chicken carcass in a pan and cover with water and bring to the boil.

2. Allow to boil for about half an hour and then remove from the pan and allow the carcass to cool.

3. Peel and chop the onions and potatoes and throw in to the pan and cook for a further 30 mins.

4. Once the carcass has cooled down pick off any meat that is left on there and add to the pan.

5. Add the peas or sweetcorn and cook another 15 mins.

A great winter warmer for those blue Mondays

Serves: 2

Calories: 342

Butternut Squash & Sweet Potato Soup

Contributed by John Joyce

Ingredients

- 1 butternut squash, cut into chunks, seeds and skin removed
- 1 sweet potato, cut into chunks, skin removed
- 2 tbsp olive oil
- 2 onions chopped
- 2 garlic cloves crushed
- 800ml hot vegetable stock (for speed I use the stock pots you can buy in the shops)
- Salt & pepper

Method

1. Add the butternut squash and sweet potato to a large pan over a medium heat with the olive oil.

2. Keep the veg moving around as it cooks.

3. Now add the chopped onions.

4. Add a small amount of the stock to prevent the veg sticking to the bottom of the pan for around 5 mins.

5. Now add the remainder of the stock, reduce the heat a little and cover with a pan lid.

6. Cook through for around 25 mins until all the veg has softened.

7. Remove from the heat and if you have a stick blender, blitz the soup. If you don't have a blender use a potato masher, gently mashing up all the veg.

8. Season to your taste with salt and pepper.

Serves: 2

Calories: 263

Serve with a bread roll or even some croutons

Greek Pork Stew

Contributed by Angie Merner

Ingredients

- 2½ lbs of pork shoulder or stewing pork
- 3lbs King Edward or Maris Piper potatoes quartered
- 2 onions
- 5 tomatoes sliced
- 1 tsp cumin
- 1 tsp cinnamon
- Olive oil

I use a more floury potato because it gives it more of a soft stew flavour and soaks up all the lovely juices more.

Method

1. Preheat oven to 200°C.

2. Fry the onions for 5 mins until soft then add the diced pork and brown for 5 mins.

3. In a large oven proof casserole dish add all the ingredients, a good drizzle of olive oil an season well with salt and pepper.

4. Place covered in the oven for around an hour then lower the heat to 180°C, remove the cover and give a gentle stir to release the juices and cook for a further 45/50 mins.

5. Serve with some fresh crusty bread and picked red cabbage.

"This is my version of a Greek pork stew I had in Rhodes a few years ago. So tasty and definitely a winter warmer. "

Serves: 6

Calories: 733

Brazilian Black Bean Stew

Contributed by Alan Paton

Ingredients

- 1 tbsp groundnut oil
- 300g chorizo, medium dice
- 300g cooked ham
- 1 medium sized onion, chopped
- 2 cloves garlic, chopped
- 2 sweet potatoes, peeled & diced
- 900g tinned, chopped tomatoes
- 1 small hot green chilli pepper
- 400ml water
- 2x 400g tins of black beans, rinsed and drained
- 1 mango, peeled & medium diced
- 50g chopped coriander

Method

1. Heat the oil in a large pot over a medium heat, place the chorizo and the ham in the pan and cook for 3 mins.

2. Place the onion in the pot and cook till tender, add the garlic and cook for 2 mins.

3. Add in the sweet potato, pepper, tomatoes, chilli and water, bring to boil and reduce heat to low - cover and simmer for 15 mins until potatoes are tender.

4. Stir the beans into the pot and cook uncovered until heated through, stir in the mango and coriander, serve.

Serves: 4

Calories: 854
Allergens: Nuts

This is a fantastic accompaniment to minced pork kebabs for a BBQ or simply a side dish – equally you could replace the meat with vegetables

44

Red Lentil Soup/Stew

Contributed by Kirsten Huesch

Ingredients

- 1 tsp oil
- 100g red lentils
- 225ml water
- ½ vegetable stock cube
- 2 tbsp tomato puree
- 1 small can sweetcorn, drained
- ½ onion, chopped
- 1-2 cloves garlic, minced
- 1 tsp curry powder (or more, depending on taste)
- Salt & pepper

Method

1. In a saucepan, heat oil and gently fry the onions and garlic until transparent.

2. Add the lentils, curry powder, water, stock cube, tomato puree and bring to the boil.

3. Turn down the heat and simmer for 30 mins, stirring frequently, until the lentils are soft.

4. Add the sweetcorn kernels and heat through.

Serve with rice, roti bread or on its own and top with a dollop of plain yogurt.

Serves: 2

Calories: 245

45

Potato Rosti

Contributed by John Joyce

Ingredients

- 1 medium potato per person
- Salt & pepper
- 2-3 tbsp olive oil for frying

Method

1. Peel the potatoes.

2. Grate the potatoes into a clean tea towel.

3. Bring the edges of the tea-towel together and squeeze over the sink to remove excess water.

4. Make sure you give the towel a good squeeze, you will be surprised how much water is removed.

5. Season the grated potato with salt and pepper.

6. Heat the olive oil over a medium heat in a large frying pan.

7. Spoon small portions of the potato into the oil, shape it into a rough circle or use a ring.

8. Don't be tempted to move them until golden and turn over.

9. Keep warm in a low heated oven whilst you fry the rest of the potato.

Serves: 1

Calories: 404

Serve with a poached egg and salad or serve as a side dish

Cheese Biscuits

Contributed by Alan Paton

Ingredients

- 100g Suffolk gold cheese
- 50g parmesan
- 100g unsalted butter
- 120g plain flour
- 1 tsp salt
- 1 tsp sugar
- Pinch cayenne
- Pinch baking powder
- 1 egg yolk

Method

1. Place all ingredients except egg into a food processor until texture is like fine breadcrumbs.

2. Add yolks and pulse this until it comes together.

3. Form dough in to long roll and wrap in cling film, chill for at least 4 hours.

4. Preheat the oven to 180°C.

5. Slice to ½ cm slices.

6. Place on baking sheet - well spaced.

7. Bake for 7 mins.

Serve with soup or as an accompaniment to salad. Alternatively try using with the Cider Rarebit *p.9*

Serves: 4

Calories: 447

Homemade Tzatsiki

Contributed by Gary Joyce

Ingredients

- 1kg natural greek yoghurt (get the greek yoghurt as it is a thicker mixture and has less water)
- 2-3 Lebanese cucumbers
- 2-3 medium-sized garlic cloves
- Olive oil
- Sea-salt flakes (not rock salt)

Serves: 4

Calories: 287

This home-made tzatsiki has been passed down from Greek generations and gives you the thick, creamy texture you will get on any Greek island holiday. The important part of this recipe is the reduction in the "liquid"

Method

1. The first thing you need to do is wash the cucumbers and cut off the ends.

2. Then get a large bowl and place a colander over the bowl. Grate the cucumbers using the large blades so you get strips of cucumber. Do this over the colander so the excess water drips through to the bowl beneath. You don't want the water in the tzatsiki otherwise the finished product is too runny.

3. Once grated cover the cucumber with paper towel to remove excess water. Leave this for a while so you can complete the other steps.

4. Take your 2-3 cloves of garlic and crush. Place in a pestle and mortar and add about 1-2 tablespoons of decent olive oil. Add a handful of salt flakes and pound and grind until the garlic is sufficiently crushed.

5. Now take another bowl and empty the contents of your Greek yoghurt. Now check on the cucumber and ensure any excess fluid is pushed through the colander by pressing down on the paper towel. Once you are happy the cucumber is relatively dry transfer to the yoghurt and stir through thoroughly. You want the mixture to look like tzatsiki.

6. When combined add the oil, salt and garlic mixture and stir through until the yoghurt has taken up the oil. You don't want the oil sitting on the yoghurt. Once the mixture is complete you can spoon back into the yoghurt container.

7. You will be left with some extra tzatsiki simply because the cucumber takes up space of some of the yoghurt. Use this excess as a dip with crackers. Put the container in the fridge and let the garlic mixture be absorbed into the yoghurt and cucumber for a few hours.

8. Take out when well chilled and serve with salads, potatoes or simply bread on its own. You will find the tzatsiki refreshing and it should have a nice thick texture to it.

9. If you like garlic then you can add more to your liking!

Smoked Mackerel Pate

Contributed by Kirsten Huesch

Ingredients

- 150g smoked mackerel (or trout), skinless
- 4 tbsp cottage cheese or Greek yogurt
- 1-2 tsp horseradish sauce (I love this but it's not essential if you hate it)
- Squeeze of lemon juice

Method

1. Simply put all the ingredients in a blender or food processor and whisk together. Adjust the seasoning once blended — you may prefer a bit more horseradish, some black pepper etc.

For a less smooth consistency, use only half the fish when blending and add the rest in flakes just before serving. You can also mash the ingredients with a fork (if you don't have a food processor or blender).

Serves: 4

Calories: 24
Alternatives:
Try using tuna
instead

Great as a sandwich/wrap filling, on toast, as a dip with crackers/crudites, on jacket potatoes...

Cheat's Honey & Mustard Mayo

Ingredients

- 3-4 tbsp mayo
- 2 tsp mustard
- 2 tsp honey

Method

1. Mix all of the ingredients together until the mayo becomes soft and coloured. This is quick and very tasty!

This recipe can complement a number of dishes within this cookbook

Serves: 8+

Calories: 31

My Real Bread

Contributed by John Joyce

Ingredients

- 500g strong white bread flour
- 350ml tepid water
- 7g sachet of dried yeast
- 1 level tbsp fine sea salt
- Flour, for dusting

Method

1. Use a large bowl to add the flour to it, make a well in the centre of the flour and pour half the water into the well. The add the yeast and stir with a fork, then add the salt and again stir with a fork.

2. Slowly, and gently, bring in the flour from the inside of the well. We don't want to break the walls of the flour to quick. Pretty soon you will be left with a stodgy, thick dough. At this point add the remaining water. I use my hands to really get amongst the dough mixture, remember this is very therapeutic, keep at it and don't panic. This is your 1st real bread dough and it won't be your last. Gradually, get all the dough together, and lightly flour your worktop. This is where you can really get aggressive with the dough.

3. Place the dough on the lightly floured worktop. Now you can start to knead the dough with a bit of elbow grease and using the ball of your palm. Be as aggressive as you wish, the harder the better and keep folding the dough back into itself. Generally this can be achieved in around 5 mins. You will notice the dough becomes more elastic and silky in its feel.

4. Flour the top of your dough. Put it in a bowl, cover with a tea towel or cling film, and allow it to prove for about 30 mins until doubled in size-ideally in a warm, moist, draught-free place. This is the time that the yeast starts to work it magic, you will notice the dough getting larger and by the time the 1st Prove is over it should have doubled in size.

5. Once your dough has doubled in size, knock the air out for 30 secs by bashing it and squashing it. Now is the time to shape it as required. I fold mine and tuck the 2 ends underneath each other and place it into one of my www.netherton-foundry.co.uk bread tins.

6. This time let it prove for a second time, around 30 mins to an hour until it has doubled in size once more. This stage is important, it gives the dough the air it needs making your loaf a really light and soft texture. It is important not to fiddle with it and let prove on its own, I tend to cover it with a clean tea towel.

7. Preheat the oven to 180°C.

8. Now it's time to bake off your bread. Gently lift the bread tin into the oven and close the door gently. Any hard knocks and you will lose all the air that has been created inside the dough.

9. I generally bake mine for 25-30 mins and keep watching it as it cooks, once it's a golden brown colour remove and check the bottom is hollow. If the bottom of the dough doesn't sound hollow enough place back in the tin and finish it off for another 5 mins.

10. Once it is cooked remove and leave on a wire rack for 30 mins to cool.

11. Now you can enjoy Real Bread with whatever you want.

I love making my own Real Bread, nothing beats it and this is just the basic recipe. Soon you will be adding your own flavours to it. Release any stress you feel by pushing the dough around.

Serves: 8

Calories: 212
Allergens: Gluten

Flatbreads

Contributed by John Joyce

Ingredients

- 7oz plain flour or wholemeal
- ¼ tsp salt
- 3½ fl oz warm water
- 2 tbsp olive oil plus extra to fry
- Optional herbs or spices you might want to add

Method

1. Put the flour and salt in a large bowl and mix to combine.

2. Add herbs or spices if you are using them.

3. Gradually add the water into the bowl.

4. Bring the mix together with your hand.

5. Add the oil and knead into the dough.

6. The aim is to create a smooth soft dough.

7. Ideally if you have the time allow the dough to stand for 30 mins.

8. Now divide the dough into 4-6 balls.

9. The fun part again, roll the balls into a disc that will fit into your frying pan.

10. Heat the pan and add a little splash of oil, similar to when you make pancakes.

11. They should take around 2 mins each side, the bread should puff up a little bit and be slightly coloured.

12. Cover the flatbreads with tin foil as you cook the others and this will keep them warm.

13. Enjoy with dips or anything you may have to use up.

Makes: 4-6

Calories: 160

54

Cucumber & Mint Riata

Contributed by John Joyce

Ingredients

- ½ cucumber
- 2 tsp mint sauce or fresh mint, chopped
- 500g greek yogurt

Method

1. Cut the cucumber in half lengthways and remove all the watery seeds. Finely chop the cucumber and add it to a bowl.

2. Now add the mint and give it a good mix. Finally add the Greek yogurt and again, give it all a good stir. Check you are happy with the flavour and adjust as required.

This version is so much better than the shop bought. Place in a serving dish and enjoy with an Indian meal or as a plain dip with nachos.

Serves: 4

Calories: 100
Allergens: Dairy
Alternatives: Dairy free yoghurt

Mango Chutney

Contributed by Sue Currie (Netherton Foundry)

Ingredients

- 4 green (under-ripe) mangoes
- 2 tsp salt
- ¼ pt malt vinegar
- ¼ pt distilled malt vinegar
- 5 oz sugar
- ½" ginger

- 10 cardamom pods
- 2 small dried chillies
- 2 tsp coriander seeds
- 1 tsp fenugreek seeds
- 1 tsp nigella seeds
- 1 muslin bag

Method

1. Peel and chop the mangoes and place in a large bowl. Sprinkle over the salt, cover with a clean tea towel and leave for 24 hours.

2. Drain and rinse the mangoes.

3. Place the vinegar, sugar and finely chopped ginger in a casserole dish or large pan.

4. Bring to the boil, then simmer for around 10 mins.

5. Add the mangoes and nigella seeds. Tie all the other spices into a muslin bag and throw that it in with the mangoes.

6. Cook gently for about 20-30 mins until the mangoes are soft and pulpy and the vinegar has virtually disappeared.

7. Taste and add more sugar, if desired.

Serves: 10

Calories: 95

56

Scotch Egg

Contributed by John Joyce

Ingredients

- 4 boiled eggs (I like my eggs to be soft boiled, then when I cut into it the yolk runs)
- 1lb sausage meat or a few sausages (skinned)
- Good dash of Worcestershire sauce
- A little flour
- 1 egg beaten
- Breadcrumbs

Method

1. Heat oven to 190°C.
2. Add the Worcestershire sauce to the sausage meat and mix well together.
3. Divide the sausage meat into 4.
4. Roll the eggs in the flour.
5. Now carefully wrap each egg in sausage meat, making sure to seal the edges together well.
6. Dip into beaten egg and then into the breadcrumbs.
7. Put on a baking tray and bake for about 25 mins.
8. Turn the scotch eggs over half way through the cooking time.

Serve hot or cold & enjoy!

Makes: 4

Calories: 489
Allergens: Egg

Salad Dressings

Contributed by John Joyce

These again are simple to make, I just use any jar with a lid to make them and give it a good shake.

French Dressing

- ¼ clove garlic crushed
- 1 tsp Dijon mustard
- 2 tbsp white or red wine vinegar
- 6 tbsp extra virgin olive oil
- 1 pinch sea salt
- 1 pinch freshly ground black pepper

Method

1. Peel, chop and crush the ¼ of a clove of garlic and place into a jar that has a lid.

2. Put Dijon mustard into the jar.

3. Now add the white or red wine vinegar.

4. Then add the extra virgin olive oil with a small pinch of sea salt and freshly ground black pepper.

5. Put the lid on the jar and shake well.

6. Use on your salad, store any that is left in the fridge.

Lemon dressing

- 6 tbsp extra virgin olive oil
- 1 pinch sea salt
- 1 pinch freshly ground black pepper
- Juice of 1 lemon

Method

1. Put the extra virgin olive oil into a jar with a lid.

2. Then add a small pinch of sea salt and ground black pepper.

3. Squeeze the juice of 1 lemon and add it to the jar.

4. Place the lid on the jar and give it a good shake.

5. Dress your salad and store any that is left in the fridge.

Balsamic dressing

- 6 tbsp extra virgin olive oil
- 2 tbsp balsamic vinegar
- 1 pinch sea salt
- 1 pinch freshly ground black pepper

Method

1. Put the extra virgin olive oil into a jar with a lid.

2. Then add a small pinch of sea salt and ground black pepper.

3. Then add the balsamic vinegar.

4. Place the lid on the jar and give it a good shake.

5. Dress your salad and store any that is left in the fridge.

Fondant Potatoes

Contributed by John Joyce

Ingredients

- 150g butter
- 4 potatoes, peeled, cut into a square or barrel shape with a knife
- 75ml chicken or vegetable stock
- 2 cloves garlic, crushed
- 2 tbsp dried thyme
- Salt & black pepper

Method

1. Heat the butter over a medium heat in a large frying pan.

2. When the butter is foaming, add the potatoes and fry until deep golden-brown on one side, about 5-6 mins (resist moving them as they brown up).

3. Turn over the potatoes and cook for a further 5-6 mins, or until golden-brown on both sides.

4. Carefully pour in the stock, then add the garlic cloves and the dried thyme (be very careful, the hot fat will splutter when it comes into contact with the stock).

5. Add salt and pepper.

6. Cover the pan with a lid and reduce the heat until the stock is simmering.

7. Simmer the potatoes until tender, then remove the potatoes from the pan gently using a slotted spoon and keep warm until you are ready to serve.

8. Enjoy with any meal of your choice.

Serves: 4

Calories: 436

These are a lovely way to enjoy potatoes, a crisp exterior with a soft centre.

60

Sauteed Potatoes

Contributed by John Joyce

Ingredients

- 600g small salad or smooth potatoes and cut in half
- 2 tbsp olive oil
- 2 cloves crushed garlic
- 2 tbsp dried rosemary

Method

1. Cook potatoes in a pan of boiling water for 4-5 mins.

2. Drain the potatoes and let them dry a little, this will help them to crisp up more.

3. Heat the oil over a medium heat in a non-stick pan.

4. Add your potatoes.

5. After a minute, add the 2 crushed garlic to the pan.

6. Stir and toss well as they cook.

7. When the potatoes are turning golden brown, add the rosemary and stir through.

8. Now when the potatoes are golden brown on all sides they're ready to serve.

9. Enjoy with any meal you make. There are so many herbs or spices you can add to make them different to suit the flavours of your dish.

Sauteed potatoes are really good to add to any meal and they are simple to achieve.

Serves: 4

Calories: 177

Runner Beans with Tomatoes & Garlic

Contributed by John Joyce

Ingredients

- 750g runner beans, sliced diagonally into 2-inch pieces
- 2 garlic cloves crushed
- 3-4 tbsp olive oil
- 12-14 tomatoes chopped into quarters
- Salt & pepper

Method

1. Cook the beans in salted boiling water until tender.

2. Drain and add to a large frying pan with the olive oil over a medium heat.

3. Toss them around and add the garlic.

4. Now add the tomatoes into the pan.

5. Give the pan a good mix and stir around.

6. Add salt and pepper to taste and reduce the heat.

7. Cook for around 10 mins.

8. Serve as a side dish.

Serves: 4

Calories: 215

You can adapt the flavours to suit you, add basil or any other herb and spice

62

Crispy Kale

Contributed by John Joyce

Ingredients

- 1 bag kale
- 2 tbsp olive oil
- Salt & pepper
  to sprinkle over

Method

1. Preheat the oven to 220°C.

2. Lay the kale on a baking tray.

3. Toss with the olive oil, salt and pepper.

4. Bake until crisp, turning the leaves halfway through.

5. The kale should be ready in around 20 mins.

Serve as a side dish or finger food with a dip

Serves: 4

Calories: 93

Spicy Baked Beans

Contributed by John Joyce

Ingredients

- 1 tbsp olive oil
- 1 onion, sliced
- ½ tsp ground cumin
- ½ tsp ground coriander
- 85g sun dried tomatoes from a jar, chopped if large

- 1 tin haricot beans
- 1 tin chopped tomatoes
- 2 tbsp balsamic vinegar
- 3-4 slices chopped bacon
- Salt & pepper

Method

1. Heat a large frying pan over a medium heat, add the oil and chopped bacon.

2. As the bacon starts to colour, add the onions and spices.

3. Now add the balsamic vinegar, giving the pan a good mix.

4. Add the tin of tomatoes, sun dried tomatoes and the haricot beans.

5. Bring to the boil and reduce the liquid a little.

6. Add salt and pepper to taste.

Serves: 2

Calories: 284

Serve with fresh toast and a fried egg

Cauliflower & Broccoli Cheese

Contributed by John Joyce

Ingredients

- 50g unsalted butter
- 50g plain flour
- 50ml semi-skimmed milk
- 500g fresh or frozen broccoli
- 75g mature cheddar cheese
- 1kg fresh or frozen cauliflower

Method

1. Preheat the oven to 180°C.

2. Add the butter to a medium pan over a medium heat.

3. When the butter has melted add the flour to make a paste.

4. Now slowly add the milk a bit at a time and whisk as you go, you want it to be smooth and silky.

5. Add the cheese and whisk through, that's the cheese sauce done.

6. In another pan add your cauliflower/broccoli and cook until the stalks go soft.

7. Now add the broccoli/cauliflower mix into an oven proof dish.

8. Cover with the cheese sauce.

9. Place in the oven and bake for around 45 mins.

To give it an extra touch, grate some fresh cheese over just before you serve

Serves: 4

Calories: 322
Allergens:
Alternatives:

Coleslaw

Contributed by John Joyce

Ingredients

- 6 tbsp plain yogurt
- ½ tsp dijon mustard
- 2 tbsp mayonnaise
- ½ white cabbage
- 2 carrots
- ½ onion

Method

1. Mix the yogurt, mustard and mayonnaise together in a bowl.

2. Now use a grater attachment on a food processor, or a box grater and grate the cabbage and carrots.

3. Either grate the onion or chop as finely as you can.

4. Now tip all of the vegetables into the bowl and stir through the dressing.

5. Add and remove any ingredients you wish to this coleslaw, this is a simple one and gives you the idea.

Serves: 4
Calories: 92

Sweet Potato Wedges

Contributed by John Joyce

Ingredients

- 2 sweet potatoes, cut into wedges
- 4 tbsp olive oil
- 1 tbsp dried thyme
- Salt & pepper to taste

Method

1. Preheat the oven to 200°C.

2. Toss the wedges with the oil and thyme then add salt and pepper.

3. Roast in the oven for 15-20 mins, until lightly browned.

4. Serve with any burger or main meal that you wish & enjoy.

These really are simple.

Serves: 2

Calories: 421

Onion Bites

Contributed by David Lewis

Ingredients

- 2 red or white onions
- Garlic salt
- 4 tbsp double cream
- 1 tbsp coarse black pepper
- 6 tsp butter

Method

1. Peel onions and cut about ½ inch thick slices (do not separate into rings).

2. Season with garlic salt.

3. Butter underside of onions.

4. Brush one side with the cream and sprinkle with the pepper.

5. Put on plate and cover loosely with foil and put it into fridge.

6. Cook on BBQ for 4-5 mins butter side down.

Serves: 4

Calories: 127

Serve as part of a BBQ buffet or on a Saturday night with chicken wings, cod bites and fries.

Potato Salad

Contributed by John Joyce

Ingredients

- 800g small new potatoes
- 3 shallots, finely chopped
- 3 tbsp mayonnaise, or to taste
- 3 tbsp extra-virgin olive oil
- 1 tbsp white wine vinegar
- Small handful parsley leaves, roughly chopped

Method

1. Boil the potatoes in salted water for 20 mins until just cooked, drain and then cool.

2. Cut the potatoes into chunks, then throw into a bowl with the shallots.

3. Add enough mayonnaise to bind, then mix together the olive oil.

4. Add just enough vinegar to give a little sharpness to the salad.

5. Finally stir in the finely chopped parsley and serve.

Nothing beats serving these with freshly cooked gammon!

Serves: 4

Calories: 242

My Sweet & Sour Sauce

Contributed by John Joyce

Ingredients

- 50g brown sugar
- 50g malt vinegar
- 130g tomato sauce or ketchup
- 1 small tin pineapple chunks in juice
- 1 tbsp light soy

Method

1. Add all your ingredients to a small pan and heat through.

2. Taste as you go and add more sweet (sugar) or sour (vinegar) if required.

Serves: 3-5

Calories: 62

Enjoy over your Chinese chicken and veg with rice

Fajita Seasoning

Contributed by John Joyce

Ingredients

- ¼ cup chilli powder
- 2 tbsp sea salt
- 2 tbsp paprika
- 1 tbsp onion powder
- 1 tbsp garlic powder
- 1 tbsp cumin powder
- 1 tsp cayenne pepper

Method

1. Mix all of the above ingredients and store in an airtight container.

2. You will only use a small portion of this mixture per serving, but it will vary on your preference for heat.

I use this for any Mexican meals I cook here. Chicken is our favourite.

Serves: 20

Calories: 16
Alternatives:
Try alternative
spices to vary
the flavour

Egg Fried Rice

Contributed by John Joyce

Ingredients

- 8oz cooked cooled boiled long grain rice
- 2 beaten eggs
- 2 tbsp toasted sesame oil
- 2 tbsp veg oil
- Any veg you may have that you want to use up

Method

1. Whisk the sesame oil with the eggs in a small bowl.

2. Add the veg oil to a frying pan over a medium heat.

3. Once the oil is hot add the rice and stir until it starts to warm through.

4. Add any veg you might want to use up to the pan and heat through, around 2-3 mins.

5. Now push all the rice mix to one side of the pan and add the egg mix.

6. I let it set a little and then stir all the rice mix through it.

Serves: 2

Calories: 510
Allergens: Egg

Serve with a curry or a sweet and sour meal.

Bread Croutons

Contributed by John Joyce

Ingredients

- Any hard bread you may have chopped into a cube shape
- 2-3 tbsp olive oil
- Any dried herbs you may have (optional)
- Salt & pepper

Method

1. Heat a large frying pan over a medium heat, add the oil and when hot add your cubed bread.

2. Season with salt and pepper and your dried herbs if using.

3. Let them go a golden colour and turn over.

4. Repeat the process, when ready serve with a soup.

You can easily let them cool down and add them to a summer salad

Serves: 6

Calories: 52
Allergens: Gluten
Alternatives:
Use gluten free
bread

Purple Sprouting Broccoli with Pink Grapefruit, Pine Nuts & Smoked Madeira Butter Sauce

Contributed by Alan Paton

Ingredients

- 16 small stems of lightly trimmed broccoli or 8 large ones blanched and cut down, you will be serving 4 pieces per person
- 1 pink grapefruit, peeled and cut into segments
- 1 tbsp pine nuts, lightly browned in the oven or under the grill. Take care not to go beyond golden or your nuts will taste bitter.

Smoked Butter Sauce:

- 8 tbsp of Madeira
- 4oz chopped butter
- 4 tbsp of double cream
- 1 tbsp of smoked oil
- Smoked sea salt to season

Serves: 4

Calories: 374

Ideal for that special occasion, or for a romantic meal by candlelight

Method

1. Reduce Madeira in pan by half.

2. Add double cream bring to boil then reduce heat to low.

3. Whisk in half the butter.

4. Now whisk in rest of butter, when half melted remove from heat and continue whisking.

5. Whisk in smoked oil, now taste it to judge how much salt you need.

6. Keep in warm place, covered.

To serve

7. Re-heat your broccoli in slightly simmering water for 10-15 secs, remove and drain, keep warm.

8. Arrange the broccoli on the plate, with the grapefruit and the nuts, finish with the sauce and an extra drizzle of smoked oil, serve.

Veggie Pasta Bake

Contributed by Rosemary Mallace

Even if you are not a vegetarian, this is a very good dish if you want to have a rest from meat.

This dish is very easy. It is made in three parts – the tomato sauce, the pasta and the cheese sauce. Cheese sauce is white sauce (béchamel) with cheese added. Don't be scared of white sauce. Once you can make white sauce a whole range of other dishes are open to you.

The tomato sauce is very forgiving and you can change and substitute the vegetables to your taste. Add garlic, leave out the celery, add more vegetables, it really is up to you. I find it is a good tasty way to use those veg that are just on the point of going off and might otherwise have been thrown out.

Try and use wholemeal pasta as it has more fibre, but ordinary, white pasta is also fine.

You will only need half the sauce that you cook here. That means you can put the rest in the fridge or freeze it for later. It can then be made into a chilli by the addition of a can of kidney beans and a few flakes of chilli. Add some root veg like swede and then top with mashed potatoes and you've got a lovely warming shepherd's pie.

Serves: 6

Calories: 522
Allergens: Egg, celery, dairy

There are many different methods of making white sauce. I have been making it for over 40 years and I find this works for me.

Ingredients

- 500g pack of passata
- 1 medium onion
- 2 medium carrots
- 1 medium pepper (any colour except green)
- 1 medium courgette
- 1 stick celery (optional)

- 200g brown lentils (make sure they are brown or green. Don't use the red lentils or it will go all mushy)
- 2 tsp dried basil
- 1 tsp salt added after the sauce is ready

Method

1. Put all the ingredients into a large pan, bring to the boil and simmer for about an hour to an hour and a half. Stir every now and then and start testing after an hour to see if it is ready. It is ready when the lentils and veg are soft (lentils do not need to be pre-soaked). If you have the time, leaving it to simmer for longer will make the sauce richer. It is very difficult to over-cook or spoil this sauce, unless you actually burn it. Meanwhile, while sauce is cooking prepare the other parts.

2. Cook 200g of pasta – doesn't matter what type, I like penne, but it is up to you.

3. Drain the pasta and run under cold water to stop it clumping together.

Cheese sauce

Ingredients

- 60g butter or margarine
- 60g flour – plain or self-raising, I find it doesn't make a difference
- 750ml milk (any type)
- 1 tsp salt – add at the end. Don't add any more because there is salt in the cheese.
- 50g strong cheese

Method

4. Preheat the oven to 200°C.

5. Melt the butter in a good sized pan – don't let it burn

6. Take pan off heat and add flour - stirring until it is a thick paste

7. Put back on heat, add the milk and stir. You need to keep stirring or it will go lumpy. It will look lumpy initially but hold your nerve and just keep stirring. You can use a hand whisk if some lumps are a bit stubborn.

8. As it comes to the boil it will start to thicken. It should be the consistency of thick cream.

9. Once it has boiled take off the heat and grate in the cheese and mix in. If you are not using it immediately, cover it so as it doesn't form a skin, although if it does, just mix it in again.

10. If the sauce is like wall paper paste, just add a bit more milk and mix it in, although you need the sauce fairly thick for this dish as the tomato sauce will thin it. Once the pasta and white sauce is ready, sit down with a gin, a glass of wine or a cup of tea and wait for the tomato sauce to be ready.

11. Once the tomato sauce is cooked, remove half of it for another day. Mix the pasta and cheese sauce into the tomato sauce and give a good mix. Transfer to an oven proof dish, top with some more cheese and pop under the grill to melt the cheese.

12. This dish can be prepared in advance and then cooked when you need it. Simply put the oven-proof dish into the fridge and put it into the oven when ready.

French Fries

Contributed by John Joyce

Ingredients

- 2-3 potatoes
- 6-8 tbsp veg oil
- Salt & pepper

Method

1. Set oven to 180°C.

2. Peel the potatoes and cut them in half (length ways) and then cut them again length ways into long thin strips. Remember you want them thicker than matchsticks.

3. Use a large frying pan with the oil over a medium heat.

4. Add the potato strips and allow them to colour up - they won't take long, give them a move around so all sides colour stay with the pan again.

5. When you are happy remove and place on an oven proof tray — I like to remove as they get a light golden colour.

6. Place in the oven for around 10 mins to cook through.

7. Remove and serve, sprinkle with salt and pepper.

Serves: 4

Calories: 253

My Vegetable Moussaka

Contributed by John Joyce

Ingredients

- 1 aubergine sliced into 1cm slices approx.
- 1 large sweet potato sliced into 1cm slices approx.
- Splash olive oil
- 1 onion thinly sliced
- 6 or 7 thinly sliced mushrooms
- 3 cloves crushed garlic
- Splash red wine
- 1 tin chickpeas
- 1 tin tomatoes
- 1 tsp oregano
- 1 tsp thyme
- 1 tsp basil
- Salt & pepper to taste
- 250-300g of grated cheese
- 2 tbsp cornflour
- 400ml milk

Serves: 4

Calories: 504

80

Method

1. Preheat the oven to 180°C

2. Lay the sweet potato and aubergine into a roasting tray, you may need 2 trays. Drizzle with olive oil, sprinkle with salt, pepper and roast in the oven until the veg takes on a little colour and remove from the oven.

3. Fry off the sliced onions over a medium heat, add the garlic and mushrooms. As soon as the pan begins to dry out add the splash of red wine. Then add the tomatoes and drain off the chickpeas and add these along with all the herbs.

4. Bring the pan back up to the boil and then simmer for around 20 mins over a low heat. Add the corn flour to the grated cheese and mix together, the flour will stick to the grated cheese.

5. Once added to the milk it will make the quickest cheese sauce I make. Heat the pan of milk, don't let it boil. You just want it to begin to bubble up, remove from the heat and add the cheese. Return the pan back to the hob and keep stirring over the heat, as the mix boils the cheese sauce will thicken and no lumps should be seen. Ok, now you are ready to build the Vegetable Moussaka.

6. Add a sweet potato layer at the bottom of an oven proof dish, then a layer of the onion, mushroom and tomato mix. On top of this add an aubergine layer and then a layer of cheese sauce. Repeat the process until you get to the top of your oven proof dish. If you have some cheese left, grate this on top of the Moussaka and bake in the oven for around 30 mins or until golden and bubbling. I always tend to watch my cooking half way through the cooking times, that way you have more control.

Stuffed Peppers with Italian Couscous

Contributed by John Joyce

Ingredients

- 250g couscous
- 1 tsp ground cumin
- 1 tsp paprika
- Salt & pepper (pinch of)
- 1 onion or shallot
- 1 large tomato
- ¼ cucumber, deseeded
- 1 tsp dried basil
- 1 tbsp lemon juice
- 2 peppers, colour of your choice
- 2 tbsp olive oil
- 2 eggs

Method

1. Preheat oven to 180°C.

2. Empty the couscous into a bowl and add the salt, pepper, cumin, paprika, basil and lemon juice. Give it all a mix around, then cover the couscous with boiling water & leave to one side until later.

3. Finely chop the onion or shallot. Cut the cucumber in half lengthways and scoop out the seeds — I use a teaspoon for this. Finely chop the tomato.

4. After 10 mins add the chopped vegetables to the cooling couscous. Give this a good mix-up again and it's ready to serve.

5. Boil the egg for approx. 4 mins. Remove from the water, drain off and leave in some cold water. Peel the shell gently. Your yolk should be nice and runny.

6. Now cut the peppers in half lengthways. Take the seeds out and place the peppers on a baking tray. Drizzle with the oil and place in the oven for around 10-15 mins.

7. When ready, remove from the oven and stuff with the couscous.

Serve with feta cheese & salad. Enjoy!

Serves: 2

Calories: 706
Alternatives:
Try mixing up the flavours by playing with different ingredients

Sweet Potato & Spinach Tortilla

Contributed by Kirsten Huesch

Ingredients

- 1 sweet potato
  (c. 125g peeled weight)
- 2 large eggs
- ½ small onion
- Little olive oil
- Large handful of fresh
  spinach leaves
- Salt & pepper
- Dash of ground paprika

Method

1. Thinly slice the sweet potato and onion and gently fry in a little oil in a small frying pan until soft.

2. Place the spinach into a sieve and pour boiling water (from the kettle) over it. Rinse with cold water to stop it wilting further, then squeeze out any liquid.

3. Add the spinach to the potato/onion in the pan.

4. Whisk the 2 eggs in a bowl together with the seasoning; pour over the potato mix and continue to cook on a low heat until you can see that the egg is almost cooked (no runny bits left).

5. Pop under the hot grill to finish off, then serve hot with a salad of your choice.

Serves: 1

Calories: 389

84

Pumpkin & Cashews

Contributed by Sue Currie

Ingredients

- 2 tbsp oil
- 4 cloves garlic
- 2 heaped tsp cumin seed
- 2 tsp salt
- ½ tsp ground cinnamon
- 1 tsp paprika
- 750g squash or pumpkin
(peeled and seeded weight), cut into chunks
- Juice of 1 orange
- 100g cashew nuts
- 2 large onions, peeled and sliced
- Dry sherry

Method

1. Preheat the oven to 180°C

2. Crush the garlic with the salt and cumin to make a paste.

3. Warm the oil in a cast iron pot and add the garlic paste, cinnamon and paprika.

4. Cook gently for a minute, then stir in the squash or pumpkin. Stir well to coat with the spice mix. Add the orange juice.

5. Put the casserole in the oven and roast for approx. 25 mins.

6. Meanwhile heat 1 tbsp oil and a knob of butter in a frying pan

7. When the butter foams, add the sliced onions and cook over a medium heat until soft and beginning to turn colour.

8. Add a splash of dry sherry and continue cooking until sticky and caramelised.

9. Remove the casserole from the oven and scatter the cashews on top - return to the oven for a further 5 mins to heat the nuts.

Serve the pumpkin and the onions on top of a bed of couscous

Serves: 3-4

Calories: 312

85

Curried Potatoes & Tomatoes with Chapatti

Contributed by John Joyce

Ingredients

- 1 potato, chopped into 1" cubes (approx.)
- 4 tomatoes, chopped into 1" pieces
- 1 tsp turmeric
- 1 tsp garam masala
- 1 tsp ground coriander
- 1 tsp crushed chilli
- 1 tsp crushed garlic
- 3-4 tbsp vegetable oil
- 2 chapattis
- Salt & pepper

Method

1. Preheat the oven to 180°C.

2. As the potatoes are chopped small, there is no need to par boil them.

3. Over a medium heat, add the oil, the potato cubes and all the spices to a large frying pan. Let it all cook for around 10 mins. The potatoes will soften and colour as they cook. Check with a sharp pointed knife that they are softening.

4. When happy, add the chopped tomatoes and give the pan a good stir/mix. The tomatoes will cook down quickly - no more than 10 mins.

5. Now place the chapatti into the hot oven for 1 min, remove and serve the curried potatoes/ tomatoes inside the chapatti and fold over.

Serves: 2

Calories: 524

Enjoy with a bowl of Cucumber & Mint Riata from the Sides & Sauces section, where you can also find the photograph for this recipe.

86

Onion Bhajis

Contributed by John Joyce

Ingredients

- Large onion, thinly sliced
- 1 pinch salt
- 2 garlic cloves crushed
- 3-4 coriander leaves chopped or 1 tbsp dried coriander
- 1 tsp turmeric
- 2 tsp curry powder
- 5 tbsp gram flour
- Water, as needed
- Oil for frying
- Salt & ground black pepper

Method

1. Place the onion in a bowl.

2. Sprinkle with the pinch of salt.

3. Mix well with your hand to separate the slices.

4. Stir in the garlic, turmeric, curry powder, and coriander leaves.

5. Stir in the gram flour, and mix by hand.

6. Add water, a little at a time until a soft dough forms.

7. The dough should not be too thick or too runny.

8. Heat the oil in a deep frying pan over high heat.

9. Drop the dough by tablespoons into the hot oil and fry until golden.

10. Remove to a plate lined with kitchen paper.

11. Season with salt and pepper.

Serves: 4

Calories: 81

Tomato & Garlic Focaccia

Contributed by John Joyce

A couple of years ago I was making these every night and they were selling as quickly as I could make them. I had one top customer who always wanted more of them. Since then I have moved into charity work, however this recipe will help that certain customer. Thanks for your feedback on these and that's why they have made #CookerySos.

Serves: 2-4
Calories: 559
Allergens: Gluten

Ingredients

- 500g strong white bread flour
- 2 tsp salt
- 2 sachets dried easy blend yeast
- 2 tbsp olive oil
- 400ml cold water
- Olive oil, for drizzling
- Handful cherry tomatoes
- 2-3 garlic cloves crushed
- Fine sea salt

Method

1. Place the flour, salt, yeast, olive oil and 300 ml of the water into a large bowl. Gently stir with your hand or a wooden spoon to form dough then knead the dough in the bowl for five mins, gradually adding the remaining water.

2. Stretch the dough by hand in the bowl, tuck the sides into the centre, turn the bowl as you go and repeat the process for about 5 mins.

3. Tip the dough onto an oiled work surface and continue kneading for five more mins. Return the dough to the bowl, cover and leave to rise until doubled in size.

4. Cut the tomatoes into slices or pieces, it's your choice and crush the garlic.

5. Line two large baking sheets with baking paper. Tip the dough out of the bowl and divide into two portions. Flatten each portion onto a baking sheet, pushing to the corners, then leave to prove for one hour.

6. Preheat the oven to 220°C. Drizzle the loaves with oil, add slices of tomato and the crushed garlic sprinkle with fine sea salt then bake in the oven for 20 mins. When cooked, drizzle with a little more olive oil and serve hot or warm.

As with all the recipes, you can add or remove the various added veg. Try roasted peppers too, the list is endless, just have fun and you won't be buying the ready-made again.

Winter Squash & Bean Chilli with Chunky Guacamole

Contributed by Steve (The Circus Gardener)

Ingredients

Chilli

- 500g winter squash, peeled & chopped into 2-3 cm cubes
- 2 medium sized onions, chopped
- 1 carrot, sliced diagonally
- 2 sticks celery, sliced diagonally
- 2 cloves garlic, finely chopped
- 1 red pepper, chopped
- 2 green peppers, chopped
- 600g tomatoes, skinned and chopped (or use equivalent weight of tinned tomatoes)
- 100g cooked kidney beans
- 100g cooked black beans
- 100g cooked chickpeas
- 30g good quality dark chocolate
- 1 tsp smoked paprika
- 1 tsp ground cumin
- 1 tsp dried oregano
- 450ml vegetable stock
- 1-2 red chillies (according to how hot you like your chilli) deseeded and finely chopped
- 1 tsp sea salt
- 2 tbsp extra virgin olive oil

Guacamole

- 2 ripe avocados, stoned, skinned and chopped finely
- 3 medium tomatoes, deskinned and chopped finely
- 1 small red onion, chopped finely
- Juice of 1 lime
- Few drops of Tabasco sauce
- 2 tbsp fresh coriander, chopped

To serve (optional, non-vegan)

- Soured cream
- Grated vegetarian cheddar cheese

Serves: 4

Calories: 771
Allergens: Celery

To serve, ladle the chilli into bowls and top with a generous tablespoonful of the guacamole. Non-vegans might also wish to top it off with a tablespoon of soured cream and some grated cheddar.

Method

1. Preheat the oven to 175°C.

2. In a large casserole dish heat the olive oil over a medium heat until hot. Add the chopped onion and cook, stirring occasionally, for 5 mins or until the onion has become soft and translucent. Add the squash, carrot, celery, chilli and garlic and stir thoroughly. Cook for a further 2 mins, stirring occasionally.

3. Now add the chopped peppers, salt, smoked paprika, cumin and oregano. Stir to combine and cook for a further min before adding the chopped tomatoes and vegetable stock. Stir and bring to a simmer.

4. Place a lid on the casserole dish and place it carefully in the preheated oven to cook for one hour. After an hour, remove from the oven, add the chocolate and stir it in thoroughly. The add the kidney beans, black beans and chickpeas and stir to combine. Replace the lid and put the chilli in the oven for a further 15 mins.

5. While the chilli is in the oven you can make the guacamole. Simply add the avocado, tomato, red onion, lime, Tabasco sauce and chopped coriander to a bowl and mix thoroughly to combine.

91

Colcannon

Contributed by John Joyce

Ingredients

- 450g potatoes
- 450g cabbage
- 2 medium leeks, trimmed, washed and thinly sliced
- 225ml milk
- Salt & pepper to taste
- 110g butter cut into small cubes

Method

1. In a large saucepan, boil potatoes until tender.

2. Scoop out and set aside. Add the cabbage and boil for 5 mins or so, until tender. Drain the cabbage and set this to one side.

3. Now add the leeks to the pot; cover with milk and simmer until soft.

4. Mash potatoes well and stir in the cooked leeks and milk.

5. Then stir in the cabbage and heat through.

6. Finally make a well in the centre of the pan and add the butter & mix all well together.

Serves: 4

Calories: 359

Serve warm and enjoy

Spiced Baked Aubergine

Contributed by John Joyce

Ingredients

- 2 aubergines
- 3 tbsp olive oil
- 1 tsp dried cumin
- 1 tsp dried coriander
- 1 tsp curry powder
- 2 onions, finely chopped
- 2 cloves garlic, crushed
- ¼ tsp chilli
- Salt & pepper
- Lemon juice

Method

1. Preheat the oven to 200°C.

2. Slice the aubergine half lengthways.

3. Make half a dozen deep diagonal slashes across each flat side.

4. Then repeat at the opposite angle to give a diamond effect.

5. Scatter the surface of each half with salt and set aside upside down for 30 mins.

6. Rinse, pat dry and place in an oven proof dish.

7. Drizzle with 1 tbsp olive oil and bake in a hot oven for around 40 mins.

8. Cook the spices with the onions and garlic on a low heat until the onions are soft.

9. Add the coriander, chilli, lemon juice and salt to the onions.

10. When the aubergines are ready, add the onion mixture over the aubergines.

Serve with a garlic bread or any dip

Serves: 2

Calories: 375

Spicy Bean Burgers

Contributed by John Joyce

Ingredients

- 2 tins kidney beans
- 1 cup breadcrumbs
- 2 beaten eggs
- 1 tsp pepper
- 1 garlic clove crushed
- 3-4 tbsp olive oil

- ½ tsp dried chilli seeds
- 1 onion finely chopped
- 1 tbsp any dried herbs you like to add, I like to use coriander in mine

Method

1. Drain the tins of kidney beans and add to a mixing bowl, squash the beans down with a fork.

2. Add the breadcrumbs, pepper, garlic and eggs plus any other flavourings you may want to use.

3. Add a little liquid if required and bring the mix together.

4. Divide the mix into 6 portions and shape them into burgers.

5. Place them into the fridge to chill for around 30 mins; this will let them firm up.

6. Heat a large frying pan over a medium heat, add the oil and add the bean burgers.

7. Don't be tempted to move them straight away; you want to get a crispy coating.

8. Turn the burgers over and repeat the process.

Makes: 6
Calories: 195

Serve in a burger bun with a slice of cheese if you wish, I like to serve with a blue cheese

94

Beetroot Curry

Contributed by Anjula Devi

Ingredients

- 4 large fresh beetroots
- 2 tbsp groundnut oil
- ½ tsp mustard seeds
- ¼ tsp ajwain
- 1tsp cumin seeds
- 1 tsp crushed coriander seeds
- 6-8 curry leaves
- 1 tbsp fenugreek leaves
- 1 medium onion - chopped finely
- 2 birds eye red chillies - slit down the middle
- 2 garlic cloves - chopped finely
- Thumbnail sized piece ginger - chopped finely
- ¼ tsp mango powder
- ¼ cup water
- 1 tsp salt
- ¼ pint of good coconut milk
- Fresh coriander —small bunch

Method

1. Wash, peel and cut the beetroot into small cubes and set aside.

2. Heat the oil on a low heat and fry the mustard seeds, ajwain, cumin seeds and coriander seeds. When the mustard seeds begin to splutter, add the curry leaves, fenugreek leaves, chopped onion, birds eye red chillies, garlic and ginger and stir. Lower the temperature and add the mango powder.

3. Add the beetroot cubes, stir well and then add the salt. Add the water, cover the pan with a lid and cook the beetroot for about 10 mins on a low heat.

4. Once the beetroot is cooked, add the coconut milk and cook for a further 10 mins without the lid on, to reduce the coconut milk down. Remove from the heat and add the chopped fresh coriander.

5. Serve with Rumali roti.

Serves: 4

Calories: 184

Garlic Tomatoes

Contributed by David Lewis

Ingredients

- 12 large red tomatoes
- 6 thyme sprigs
- 12 garlic cloves
- ¼ cup olive oil

Method

1. Preheat oven to 220°C.

2. Cut tomatoes in half and in baking dish (casserole dish is best) place cut side up.

3. Arrange unpeeled garlic cloves and three thyme sprigs among tomatoes. Drizzle oil over.

4. Put in oven at 220°C uncovered for about 40 mins (tomatoes should just be darkening).

5. Take out oven and throw away cooked thyme.

6. Use the cooked garlic to squeeze on to tomatoes.

7. Put the three fresh thyme sprigs on top and serve.

Serves: 4

Calories: 220

Can be cooked days before and reheated for 5 mins on the day

96

Steak & Tomatoes

Contributed by John Joyce

Ingredients

- 2 rump steaks
- 6-8 tomatoes cut in half
- 6-8 mushrooms cut in half
- 1 onion sliced
- 1 tbsp balsamic vinegar
- 3-4 tbsp olive oil
- Salt & pepper

Method

1. In a large frying pan add 2 tbsp of oil on a medium heat.

2. Season the steaks both sides with the salt and pepper, then add them to the pan and turn the heat up; cook for 2-3 mins each side.

3. Remove from the pan and leave on a plate to one side.

4. Add remainder of the oil, then add the halved tomatoes, sliced onions and mushrooms.

5. Let all the vegetables infuse and the tomatoes colour.

6. Add the balsamic vinegar; now add salt/pepper to taste.

7. Cut the steaks into nice size strips — you choose how small/wide you want them.

8. Add the steak and juice from the plate back to the pan with the vegetables.

9. Now cook through all together, 2-3 mins should do.

10. When you are happy removed and plate up.

I served mine with French fries. Your choice. Enjoy!

Serves: 2

Calories: 332

Cottage Pie

Contributed by John Joyce

Ingredients

- 400g lean minced beef
- 2 medium onions, chopped
- 2 celery sticks, finely sliced
- 2 medium carrots, diced
- 400g can chopped tomatoes
- 2 tbsp tomato purée
- 500ml beef stock
- 1 tbsp Worcestershire sauce
- 1 tsp dried mixed herbs
- 4 tsp cornflour
- 1 tbsp cold water
- Salt & pepper
- 750g floury potatoes
- 150g milk

Serves: 4

Calories: 393
Allergens:
Celery, dairy

Enjoy! You could use sweet potatoes for the topping or even curry up the cottage pie. The choice is yours

Method

1. In a large non-stick saucepan or flameproof casserole dish over a medium heat. Add the mince and cook it with the onions, celery and carrots for 10 mins until lightly coloured. Use a wooden spoon or spatula to break up the meat as it cooks.

2. Stir in the tomatoes, tomato purée, beef stock, Worcestershire sauce and mixed herbs. Season with a good pinch of salt and plenty of freshly ground black pepper. Bring to the boil, then reduce the heat, cover loosely and simmer gently for 40 mins, stirring occasionally until the mince is tender.

3. About 20 mins before the meat is ready, make the potato topping. Peel the potatoes and cut them into rough 4cm chunks. Put them in a large saucepan and cover with cold water. Bring to the boil, then turn down the heat slightly and simmer for 18-20 mins or until the potatoes are very tender. Drain the potatoes, then tip them back into the pan, season to taste and mash with the milk and a dash of butter until smooth.

4. Preheat the oven to 220°C. When the beef has been simmering for 40 mins, mix the cornflour with the cold water to make a smooth paste. Stir this into the beef and cook for another 1-2 mins or until the sauce is thickened, stirring often.

5. Pour the beef mixture into a 2-litre shallow ovenproof dish. Using a large spoon, top the beef with the mashed potatoes. Spoon the mixture all around the edge of the dish before heading into the middle, then fluff up with a fork.

6. Bake for 30 mins until the topping is golden and the filling is bubbling.

Short Beef Ribs

Contributed by John Joyce

Ingredients

- 2lb 4oz short beef ribs
- 2 tbsp olive oil
- 2 carrots, peeled, cut into pieces
- 1 large onion, peeled, thickly sliced
- 5 garlic cloves, peeled
- 2-3 sprigs fresh thyme
- 400g canned chopped tomatoes
- 350ml red wine
- 200ml beef stock
- Salt & freshly ground black pepper

Method

1. Preheat the oven to 170°C.

2. Heat the oil in a large roasting tray or casserole pan over a medium to high heat.

3. Add the beef ribs and fry, turning regularly, until browned on all sides.

4. Add the carrots, onion and garlic and stir until coated in the oil and pan juices.

5. Add the thyme sprigs, and then pour in the chopped tomatoes, red wine and beef stock and mix all well to combine.

6. Bring the mix to the boil and then place into the oven.

7. Cook, uncovered, for 2-2½ hours, or until the sauce has thickened and the meat is falling from the bones.

8. Add salt and freshly ground black pepper to suit your taste.

9. Serve with mashed potatoes and a side serving of veg to your preference.

Serves: 4

Calories: 1074

100

Chilli Con Carne

Contributed by John Joyce

Ingredients

- 1 onion finely chopped
- 1 stick celery, finely chopped
- 2 tbsp olive oil
- 500g minced beef
- 3 garlic cloves crushed
- 1 red pepper chopped
- 2 chopped red chillies deseeded

- 1 tin chopped tomatoes
- 300ml beef stock
- 1 tin kidney beans, drained
- Salt & pepper
- 1 tbsp tomato puree
- 1 tsp oregano

Method

1. Put a pan on the hob and get it really hot and add the oil.

2. Add the mince and brown it really well breaking it up as it cooks.

3. Remove from the pan and strain if needed.

4. Put a little olive oil in the pan add the onion , celery , pepper and cook over a medium heat for about 15 mins without browning.

5. Add the tomato purée and cook it out for a few mins.

6. Add the meat back to the pan and combine well.

7. Add the chilli, oregano red pepper, stir well.

8. Cook for another 5 mins season well.

9. Add the tin of tomatoes stir and cook for another 5 mins.

10. Pour in the stock, bring up to a simmer then turn the heat down and let it cook gently for 40-45 mins.

11. Stir it occasionally.

12. Add the beans, leave for another 10 mins.

Serve with rice or wedges

Serves: 4

Calories: 449
Allergens: Celery

Bolognese

Contributed by John Joyce

Ingredients

- 2 tbsp olive oil
- 500g beef mince
- 2 small onions, chopped
- 2 cloves garlic, crushed
- 2 tins tomatoes
- 2-3 tbsp dried Italian herbs
- 1 tbsp tomato puree
- 1 tbsp balsamic vinegar
- 250g mushrooms chopped

Method

1. Put a pan on the hob and get it really hot and add the oil.

2. Brown your meat and fry your onions.

3. Add your mushrooms and garlic .

4. Add the tomatoes and rinse out the can with water and add it to the pan.

5. Now add the herbs to the mix.

6. Add your tomato puree.

7. Then add balsamic vinegar.

8. Add salt and pepper.

9. Leave to simmer for at least 1 hour and then taste.

10. Add more seasoning if required.

Serves: 4

Calories: 337

Serve with pasta or a jacket potato

Braised Steak with Vegetables

Contributed by Garmon Owen

Ingredients

- Braising steak (one each)
- 2-3 potatoes
- 2-3 carrots
- 2 onions
- 1 stock cube (e.g. Oxo)
- 1 pint boiling water

Method

1. Preheat oven to 160°C.

2. Coat the steaks in flour and fry both sides in a little oil to brown. Use an oven proof tin with a lid and take off the heat.

3. Peel and chop the onions and add.

4. Peel and chop potatoes and carrots and add to the tin.

5. Dissolve the stock cube in the boiling water and add to the mix.

6. Cover and place in the oven for 2 hours.

Job done. Simply plate up and enjoy with a slice of Real Bread

Serves: 1

Calories: 488

Chinese Style Ribs

Contributed by John Joyce

Ingredients

- 8-10 spare ribs, this is based on 2 people, adjust for your family needs
- 150g hoisin sauce
- 2 tbsp light soy sauce
- 2 tbsp honey
- 3 tbsp five spice
- 1 tbsp tomato puree
- 3-4 tbsp olive oil

Method

1. Preheat the oven to 200°C.

2. Cook the ribs in a pan of boiling water until tender but the meat isn't dropping off.

3. Mix all the ingredients above in a bowl and then dress the ribs in it.

4. Make sure all the ribs receive the coating.

5. Add the ribs to an oven proof dish or tray .

6. Place in the oven until golden and the ribs have become sticky.

Serves: 2

Calories: 629
Allergens: Clove

Enjoy as a side dish or serve with egg fried rice or any BBQ food.

Dan's Chicken Stir Fry

Contributed by Daniel McDonald

Ingredients

- 1 tbsp oil
- 2 skinless/boneless chicken fillets
- 2 medium carrots
- ¼ savoy cabbage
- 3 sticks of celery
- 1 large leek
- Soy sauce (to taste)
- Sweet chilli sauce (to taste)

Method

1. Cut the chicken fillets into bite sized pieces.

2. Heat the oil in a wok and add the chicken, cook until the chicken is sealed.

3. Meanwhile shred the Savoy cabbage, chop the carrots and leeks into matchstick sized pieces and the celery into 1cm pieces.

4. Add the vegetables and soy sauce, to the chicken and cook until the chicken is cooked through.

5. Finally add enough sweet chilli sauce to taste and stir through.

6. Serve on a bed of rice or noodles.

Vegetables can be varied according to your taste.

Serves: 2

Calories: 273
Allergens: Celery

Homemade Goan Chicken Curry Puff Parcels with Lime & Coriander Couscous

Contributed by Rosalind Tsang

Ingredients

Filling:

- 1 large chicken breast (or leftover chicken from a roast), sliced or small chunks
- Sauce (can be a jar & any flavour you like -doesn't have to be goan inspired)
- 400ml can coconut milk
- 1 tbsp vegetable or olive oil
- 1 medium onion chopped
- ½ carrot and courgette chopped
- 1 tsp yellow or brown mustard seeds
- Bunch of coriander chopped

Pastry:

- Puff pastry 320g (shop bought is fine)
- 1 egg yolk
- 2 tbsp sesame seeds

Marinade:

- 1" finely chopped ginger
- 3 cloves garlic crushed
- 1½ tsp ground coriander
- 1 tsp ground cumin
- 1 tsp paprika
- 1 tsp chilli powder (or to taste)
- 1 tsp sugar
- ½ tsp turmeric
- ½ lime
- ½ tsp salt & pepper
- Pinch thyme & oregano

Couscous:

- 200g couscous
- ½ lime
- Handful coriander, chopped
- Sultanas
- 10cm cucumber chopped
- 1 fresh chopped tomato
- Salt & pepper

Method

1. Preheat the oven to 200°C. Ensure to keep the pastry cool until use.

2. Marinade the chicken for 20 mins or combine the chicken with your chosen sauce.

3. Heat the oil in a pan or wok, add mustard seeds, cook for about 1 min until they start to pop.

4. Fry the chicken with the rest of the marinade/sauce to release the flavours then add the rest of the sauce ingredients for 10 mins until softened and then add the coconut milk. Bring to a simmer and cook for 15 mins until thickened, taste and season accordingly.

5. Allow the mixture to cool before using with the pastry.

6. To make the parcels unroll the pastry and divide into 12 squares. Spoon the cooled chicken curry filling into the centre of a pastry square. Pinch two opposite corners together then continue to pinch and seal the pastry into a triangle shape. Crimp the edges with a fork and repeat until complete.

7. Brush the egg yolk over the pastry parcels then sprinkle on the sesame seeds.

8. Bake on the middle shelf in the oven for 25-30 mins until puffed golden and crispy, serve with the couscous and a dollop of mint yoghurt.

Serves: 6

Calories: 668

Easy Paprika Chicken Salad

Contributed by Kirsten Huesch

Ingredients

- 2 chicken breasts, cut into finger-thick slices
- 2 tsp paprika powder
- Salt, pepper
- Knob of butter
- Lettuce
- Any other salad ingredients you may have such as cucumber, cherry tomatoes, radishes, spring onions, peppers etc.

For the dressing

- 2 tbsp olive oil
- ½ tbsp balsamic vinegar
- ½ tsp mustard
- 1 clove garlic, crushed
- Salt & pepper
- Optional: dried herbs e.g. basil, oregano or some fresh chilli

Method

1. Season the chicken pieces with salt and pepper and liberally sprinkle with paprika powder.

2. Heat a frying pan over a medium heat, add the butter and once melted and sizzling, add the chicken pieces.

3. Turn frequently and cook until done (6-7 mins should suffice), then set aside whilst mixing up the dressing in a small jar or bowl.

4. Assemble your salad ingredients on two plates and top with the chicken pieces, then drizzle with the dressing.

Serves: 2

Calories: 477

Serve on its own or with crusty bread.

Thyme Chicken with Rice

Contributed by Kirsten Huesch

Ingredients

- 300g chicken thighs (breast also works)
- 2 heaped tsp cornflour
- 1 tbsp oil
- 200g leeks, sliced
- 1 clove garlic, crushed
- 200ml stock (vegetable or chicken, made from a cube & water)
- 1 heaped tsp dried thyme
- 2 tbsp double cream or reduced-fat evaporated milk

Method

1. Cut the chicken into bite-size chunks and dust evenly with cornflour.

2. In a pan, heat 1 tbsp oil and when hot, add the chicken, leeks and garlic. Fry for a couple of mins, then reduce the heat.

3. Now add the stock and dried thyme and leave to simmer for 10-15 mins.

4. Finish off by adding the cream (or evaporated milk) and adjust the seasoning (if necessary) by adding salt and pepper. Serve on vegetable rice.

You can also use this as a quick & easy filling for a chicken pie. Use slightly less stock (maybe 100ml) to make the filling drier, spoon into a pie dish and cover with a thin layer of puff pastry (I use ready-made puff pastry for this). Brush the pastry with milk or beaten egg and bake in the oven at 180°C (fan oven) until the pasty is golden - it should be ready in 15-20 mins (but please check the instructions if using ready-made).

Serves: 2

Calories: 566

Chicken Escalope

Contributed by John Joyce

Ingredients

- 1 lemon
- Breadcrumbs
- 4 sprigs fresh or dried parsley
- Sea salt
- Freshly ground black pepper

- 2 heaped tbsp all-purpose flour
- 1 large free-range egg
- 2 skinless chicken fillets
- 2-3 tbsp olive oil

Method

1. Add breadcrumbs to a large bowl.

2. Zest the lemon into the bowl.

3. Finely chop the fresh parsley and add this, if it's the dried variety add a couple of tsp of it.

4. Give all of the bowl a good mix and add a little salt and pepper, again mix through.

5. Now add the flour to another plate and spread across evenly.

6. Crack the egg onto another small plate and give it a quick beat with a fork.

7. Now wrap the chicken fillets into cling wrap, use a rolling pin or similar to flatten out the chicken. This is another area where you can release stress without realising it.

8. Don't beat them into total submission, just enough to flatten them out.

9. Dip the chicken into the flour and then into the egg and lastly the flavoured bread crumbs.

10. Make sure the chicken is covered in the breadcrumb, if needed give it a little push down.

11. Heat a pan over a medium heat, add the olive oil and cook the fillets for around 4-5 mins on each side. You want them to be golden and crisp.

12. Serve with fresh salad or potato wedges

Serves: 2

Calories: 509

Beer Can Chicken

Contributed by John Joyce

Ingredients

- 1 can beer or lager
- 1 tsp chilli powder
- 1 tsp English mustard powder
- 1 tsp crushed garlic
- 1 tsp smoked paprika
- 1 tsp muscovado sugar
- 1 chicken
- Pinch salt

Method

1. For the chicken, mix half of the beer or lager, chilli powder, mustard, garlic, smoked paprika, and sugar together in a bowl to make a paste.

2. Rub the paste all over the chicken and set aside to marinate for as long as you can in the fridge.

3. Preheat the oven to 190°C.

4. Now carefully lift the chicken onto the beer can so the chicken is sitting upright with the can in its cavity.

5. The remainder of the beer or lager will create steam inside the cavity and the chicken meat will be nice and moist.

6. Keep an eye on the chicken and after 40-45 mins your chicken should be ready. Remove and set aside to allow the meat to rest.

7. Enjoy with wedges, potatoes,... the list is endless.

Serves: 5

Calories: 99

Easy Black Pepper Chicken Wings

Contributed by Laura Stonehouse

This recipe is Low-FODMAP, gluten-free and dairy-free. Pop into Our House For Tea for more Low-FODMAP mealtimes. www. ourhousefortea.com

I love my butchers. Six years ago I didn't really have a specific butcher but once I got over my initial fear of talking to them I haven't looked back! I'm no good with weights and measures but I soon realised I could simply ask them how much they thought I needed, after all, they are the experts. They can advise on what cut I should get, what the most affordable option is and how to cook it.

I order my wings the day before I need them so they have time to prep them. With limited strength in my right hand, I find it difficult to find chop off the wing tips. I ask for these to be removed for me and saved to make stock, but if you can't get any wings ready 'tipped' it really isn't a problem.

Serves: 6

Calories: 662

Eat with fingers and bask in the thought of not washing up cutlery.

Ingredients

- 2kg chicken wings (around 20 wings)
- 1 tbsp. olive oil
- 2 limes
- ½ lemon

- 1 tsp black peppercorns crushed in a pestle and mortar, or, ½ tsp course ground black pepper
- ½ tsp salt flakes

Method

1. In a large roasting tin, place the oil and pepper then squeeze in the juice of the limes and lemon. Let any pieces of the flesh that come free fall into the tin too. Tip the pan so the juices all come together and lightly mix together using a small whisk or fork.

2. Place the chicken into the pan and, using your hands, turn over in the marinade until everything is well coated. Squeeze the meat into an even layer. Cover and leave to marinate for a minimum of 30 mins, maximum 10 hours in a cold place (below 4.4°C, ideally in a fridge). Preheat the oven° to 200°C Add the salt flakes, turn over the wings in the marinade and bake for 40 mins, turning the wings over after 20 mins.

3. Eat with fingers and bask in the thought of not washing up cutlery.

Spatchcock Chicken

Contributed by John Joyce

Ingredients

- 1 chicken, spatchcocked (ask your butcher to do this for you)
- Juice 1 lemon
- 2 tsp mild chilli powder
- 85g natural yogurt
- 85g coconut cream
- 3 garlic cloves, crushed
- 1 tsp ginger
- 1 tbsp tomato purée
- 1 tsp ground cumin
- 1 tsp dried coriander
- 1 tsp garam masala
- 1 tsp turmeric
- 1 tbsp olive oil

Method

1. Preheat the oven to 220°C.

2. Place the chicken in a large dish and slash the legs a few times with a sharp knife.

3. Mix together the lemon juice, chilli powder and 1 tsp salt.

4. Now pour this over the chicken, turning so that it coats both sides.

5. Cover with cling film and chill in the fridge for 1 hour.

6. Mix all the remaining ingredients (except the oil) and some black pepper in a bowl until smooth (if you have a blender use this).

7. Remove the chicken from the fridge and rub the spicy paste all over the chicken.

8. Place the chicken on to a oven proof tray or dish and place in the oven.

9. Cook for at least 20 mins, if the top of the chicken is colouring too quick cover with foil.

10. Turn the chicken over and cook again for another 20 mins.

11. Now turn the chicken back over and let the colour deepen for around 5-10 mins.

12. Remove and allow to rest for around 10 mins.

13. Serve with a fresh salad or any dips or even a chutney.

Enjoy and play around with the spices

Serves: 4

Calories: 139

Chicken Casserole

Contributed by John Joyce

Ingredients

- 4 chicken fillets
- 1 tbsp oil
- 2 onions, sliced
- 10-12 button mushrooms
- 2 tbsp plain flour
- 2 chicken stock cubes
- 2 large carrots, cut into slices
- 400g new potatoes, cut into half if large
- 200g frozen peas
- 1 tin tomatoes
- 2 bay leaves
- 2 tbsp tarragon

Method

1. Boil a kettle of water.

2. Fry the thighs in the oil in a casserole or wide pan with a lid to quickly brown.

3. Add the sliced onions, mushrooms the flour and stock cubes until the flour disappears.

4. Now slowly stir in 750ml hot water from the kettle.

5. Add the carrots, potatoes, tomatoes and tarragon and bring to a simmer.

6. Cover and cook for 20-30 mins.

7. Remove the lid and simmer for 15 mins more.

8. Finally add the peas for another 5 mins.

9. Add salt and pepper to taste. Serve and enjoy.

Serves: 3-4

Calories: 495

Chicken Curry

Contributed by Jason Woods

Ingredients

- 2 medium onions
- 1 whole bulb garlic
- 1" ginger
- 50g tomato paste
- 4 chicken thighs
- Cumin seeds
- Coriander seeds

- Chilli powder
- Coriander powder
- Cumin powder
- Cinnamon powder
- Fresh mint/coriander
- Salt & pepper
- Sunflower oil

Method

1. Heat seeds in oil.

2. Add peeled and chopped onion, garlic and ginger. Cook gently. Add tomato paste and cook through.

3. Add a teaspoon of each powder and stir as it cooks to a paste.

4. Add water if it needs thinning out.

5. Add chicken thighs, either boned or on the bone depending on choice and cook for approx 20 mins.

6. Season. Add fresh chopped herbs and serve!

Notes and variations.

7. Use diced beef or lamb or favourite vegetables.

Don't worry too much about exact measurements. Be guided by your senses. A 'masala' is just a name for the blend of spices.

Serves: 4

Calories: 210

Tandoori Chicken in a Chapatti

Contributed by John Joyce

Ingredients

- 2 chicken fillets
- 1 lemon
- Salt & pepper
- 250g plain greek yogurt
- 6-8 tbsp tandoori spice
  – Asian Shop Spice is best
- 1 tin chopped tomatoes
- Fresh coriander
- 1 onion, sliced or chopped
- 2 cloves of garlic, finely crushed
- 2 chapattis
  – shop-bought or homemade

Serves: 2

Calories: 824

I generally cook this as one of my "Saturday night finger food" meals. It's easy and tasty – never mind the take-away!

Method

1. Using a small sharp knife cut the chicken fillets into pieces – size depends on you. I tend to cut them into goujon size.

2. In a bowl, whisk together the yogurt, lemon juice, tandoori spice and add the chicken.

3. Cover in cling wrap and place in the fridge for a couple of hours.

4. Chop the onion and add to a wok or large frying pan over a medium heat until they turn a nice golden brown colour and remove from the pan.

5. Add the chicken and cook over a medium heat so it begins to catch a deep rich colour. Then add the chopped tomatoes and onions back into the pan.

6. Add a little salt and pepper to taste.

7. Finally add the garlic, stirring occasionally. The aim is to reduce the liquid in the pan. All the time the chicken will soak up all the flavours. You want a dry mixture to place in the chapattis.

8. Turn the oven to approx. 200°C and place your chapattis in the oven. These just want warming through – about 5 mins should be fine.

9. Now everything is ready! Place some of the tandoori chicken in your chapatti. Chop up a bit of the fresh coriander and sprinkle on the chicken. Fold over the chapatti and enjoy!

Tandoori Chicken Kebabs

Contributed by John Joyce

Ingredients

- 3-4 BBQ skewers – soaking in cold water
- 2 chicken fillets
- 1 lemon
- Salt & pepper
- 250g plain Greek yogurt
- 6-8 tbsp tandoori spice - Asian Shop Spice is best
- 3-4 tomatoes
- Fresh coriander
- 1 green or red pepper
- 4-6 mushrooms
- 2 cloves garlic, finely crushed
- 2 tbsp olive oil

Method

1. Set the oven to 200°C.

2. Using a small sharp knife cut the chicken fillets into pieces – size depends on you. I tend to cut them into goujon size.

3. In a bowl, whisk together the yogurt, lemon juice, tandoori spice, garlic and add the chicken.

4. Cover in cling wrap and place in the fridge for a couple of hours.

5. Now cut the onion into nice wedge pieces, mushrooms in half and the pepper into big wedges. Similar to how you do your BBQ skewers in the summer.

6. Now it's time to make your Tandoori Chicken Kebabs. Remove the chicken and start to push the meat onto the skewer. Alternate with the chopped veg and be as adventurous as you want.

7. Heat the oil in a large frying pan over a medium heat. Place the skewers into the oil and allow to colour, as they do give them a turn over. Any scolding of the meat and veg will add to the flavour, just don't burn them to a crisp.

8. Once you have turned them and they look ready remove and place on a baking tray. Place them into the oven to cook through. This process should take no longer than 10 mins.

9. Add to your plate and dress up with freshly chopped coriander. This is another Saturday night finger food meal. Quick and simple but plenty of flavour.

Serve with rice or wedges if you wish.

Serves: 2

Calories: 840
Allergens: Dairy

121

Chicken Stir Fry

Contributed by John Joyce

Ingredients

- 4 chicken fillets (cut into strips)
- 1 tsp ginger
- 1 red pepper
- 1 shallot
- 1 clove garlic, crushed
- 1 red chilli (optional deseeded and chopped)
- 1 tbsp vegetable oil
- 1 tbsp fish sauce
- Juice of 1 lime

Method

1. Heat a wok and pour in 1 tbsp oil.
2. Cook the chicken for 7-10 mins.
3. Keep the chicken moving about until cooked.
4. Then put to one side.
5. If required add another 1 tbsp of oil.
6. Add the pepper and cook for 1 min.
7. Now cook the ginger, shallot and garlic for 1-2 mins more.
8. Combine the fish sauce and lime juice.
9. Add this into the wok, then add the chicken back in
10. Cook for 1 min, serve with the rice.

Serves: 2

Calories: 631

Chinese Chicken Stuffed Peppers

Contributed by John Joyce

Ingredients

- 1 red pepper
- 2 chicken fillets, cut into strips
- 2 tsp five spice
- 2 cloves garlic, chopped
- 1 tbsp dark soy sauce
- ½ fresh chilli or 1 tsp dried chilli
- 2 tbsp olive oil
- 1 onion chopped
- 6-8 mushrooms, chopped

Method

1. Set the oven to 180°C.

2. Cut the pepper in half lengthways and remove the seeds. Leave the stem in if you can – this will give it a nice look on the plate.

3. Place the two halves on a baking tray and place in the oven. Keep an eye on them until they start to soften a little and remove.

4. Now add the chicken into a pan with the oil over a medium heat. Allow it to brown up a little, then add onions, mushrooms and spices along with the soy sauce. Give the pan a good stir, making sure everything has a good mix.

5. When the chicken is ready, spoon into the peppers and place back into the oven to warm through – no more than 10 mins.

6. Serve on their own or with rice or chips.

Serves: 1

Calories: 890

123

Chinese Chicken & Noodles

Contributed by John Joyce

Ingredients

- 2 chicken fillets
- 1 tsp five spice
- 1 tbsp olive oil
- 1 tbsp sesame oil
- 1 tsp sweet chilli sauce
- 2 blocks egg noodles
- 2 good handfuls beansprouts
- 4 spring onions
- 1 pack baby corn
- 1 pack mange tout
- 1 tbsp soy sauce
- Salt & pepper

Method

1. Slice and marinade your chicken in the 5 spice, sesame oil and sweet chilli sauce.

2. In a pan of boiling water soften your noodles for 3 mins. Drain and drizzle in a little of the olive oil and toss well.

3. In a hot wok over a high heat, fry your chicken for around 5 mins.

4. Add your veg and fry for a further 5 mins.

5. Add the noodles and soy sauce and fry for another 2-3 mins, tossing them about well.

6. Season with salt and pepper to taste.

7. Add the beansprouts and fry for around 1 min.

Serves: 2
Calories: 707

Serve and enjoy!

Teriyaki Chicken

Contributed by John Joyce

Ingredients

- 2 chicken fillets cut into strips
- 3-4 tbsp teriyaki sauce
- 1 thumbsized piece of chopped ginger (or dried)
- 2 chopped garlic cloves
- 2 tbsp olive oil
- 2 tbsp honey
- Salt & pepper
- 2 tbsp water

Method

1. Add the teriyaki sauce, ginger, garlic, 1 tbsp olive oil, honey and 1 tbsp of water to a dish.

2. Give all the ingredients a good mix. Now add the chicken strips into the dish.

3. Again give this a good stir/mix, the aim is to cover the chicken with the marinade.

4. Cover with cling film and leave in the fridge for 15 mins or longer if you can.

5. Now heat a frying pan over a medium heat and add the remainder of the olive oil. Remove the chicken from the fridge, pick out the strips of chicken and add to the pan. Fry them off over a medium heat and turning over as required.

6. Add any remaining marinade to the pan and heat through, now reduce the liquid and watch how sticky the chicken becomes due to the honey.

7. Serve with a fresh salad or rice.

Serves: 2

Calories: 489

Piri-Piri Chicken

Contributed by John Joyce

Ingredients

- 4 tbsp olive oil
- 1 tbsp honey
- 2 tsp paprika
- 2 tsp chopped coriander leaf
- 2 crushed cloves of garlic

- 1 lemon, juiced
- 2 chicken fillets, cut into strips
- 1 tbsp crushed chilli or fresh if you have them
- Salt & pepper

Method

1. Add the oil, paprika, coriander leaf, garlic, lemon juice and chilli together with the honey to a bowl or dish. Then add the chicken strips to the mix and give everything a good stir around. Make sure the chicken gets a good coating.

2. Cling wrap and place in the fridge. I left mine for an hour. When ready, remove from the fridge and add the chicken strips to a large frying pan. Cook over a medium heat and allow to cook through. Don't worry if some of the chicken begins to get scorched a little – this adds to the flavour.

Serves: 2

Calories: 575

I serve mine in a wrap with salad – the choices are endless... you may prefer potato wedges.

126

 Thai Curry

Contributed by John Joyce

Ingredients

- 1 small onion finely chopped
- 1 stalk lemongrass finely sliced
- 1 tbsp vegetable oil
- 3-4 tsp red Thai curry paste
- 4 chicken breasts, cut into bite-size pieces

- 1 tbsp fish sauce
- 1 tsp sugar, brown is best
- 4 kaffir lime leaves
- 400ml can coconut milk
- 20g pack fresh coriander

Method

1. Heat the oil in a wok or large frying pan for a couple of mins.

2. Add the onion.

3. Fry for 3-5 mins until soft and translucent.

4. Stir in the curry paste and cook for 1 min stirring all the time.

5. Add chicken pieces and stir until they are coated.

6. Now add the lemongrass, fish sauce, sugar, kaffir lime leaves and coconut milk.

7. Bring slowly to the boil, then reduce heat and simmer, uncovered, for 15 mins until the chicken is cooked.

8. Stir the curry a few times while it cooks, to stop it sticking and to keep the chicken submerged.

Serve with rice

Serves: 2

Calories: 734

Chicken Enchiladas

Contributed by John Joyce

Ingredients

- 2 skinless, boneless chicken breast fillets
- 2-3 tbsp olive oil
- 1 onion, chopped
- 6-8 mushrooms chopped
- 225ml soured cream
- 125g grated Cheddar cheese
- 1 tbsp dried parsley
- ½ tsp dried oregano
- ½ tsp ground black pepper
- ½ tsp salt (optional)
- 400g passata
- 125ml water
- 1 tbsp chilli powder
- Chopped green or red pepper
- 1 clove garlic, minced
- 8 flour tortillas
- 300g salsa or enchilada sauce
- 65g grated Cheddar cheese

Method

1. Preheat oven to 180°C.

2. Heat a large frying pan over a medium heat on the hob.

3. Cook the chicken until it has a bit of colour and the juices run clear.

4. Remove and add the onion, mushrooms, pepper, parsley, oregano, black pepper and garlic.

5. Soften and add the soured cream and 125g grated cheese.

6. Once the cheese has melted add the passata, water, chilli powder.

7. Heat through and leave to one side.

8. Now roll even amounts of the chicken mix into the tortillas.

9. Lay them in an oven proof dish.

10. Cover with the salsa or enchilada sauce and cover with the cheese.

11. Now bake off the enchiladas in the oven for around 20-25 mins.

12. Allow to cool for around 10 mins and serve with a fresh salad or garlic bread.

Enjoy, this is one of my favourite meals.

Serves: 4

Calories: 616

Salmon on a bed of Leeks with Sautéed Potatoes & Lemon Sauce

Contributed by John Joyce

Ingredients

- 2 tbsp olive oil
- 2-3 medium sized potatoes
- 1 leek
- 2 salmon fillets
- 1 lemon or lemon juice

- 25g butter
- 25g plain flour
- 200ml milk
- Sea salt & pepper

Method

1. Peel the potatoes and cut into small sized cubes. If they are too big, they will need part boiling. I keep them small as they fry off and soften quicker.

2. Melt the butter and add the flour - beat with a wooden spoon over a low/medium heat. Once the mix has thickened add the milk slowly, a bit at a time. Keep stirring and then use a whisk to beat it smooth. Once happy with the texture, add the juice of a lemon.

3. Add your potatoes in a wok or frying pan with a tbsp of olive oil over a medium heat. Watch them as they cook and keep moving the pan/turn the potatoes over until they are golden.

4. In another pan add the remainder of the oil over a medium heat. Season the salmon with salt and pepper and add to the pan. Watch as the salmon colour changes as it cooks through.

5. If required, turn the salmon over gently and let the top brown up - a couple of mins should do. Turn the salmon back over and add a small knob of butter to the pan. Drizzle this over the salmon as it cooks. When you are happy, remove from the heat.

6. Chop the leek up into slices. Add to a pan with a little oil and a dash of water over a medium heat. Add a pinch of salt and pepper and fry off. As the leeks wilt and soften, they will turn a light golden colour.

7. Now all should be cooked and ready to plate up. Drizzle over your lemon sauce and enjoy!

Salmon has a number of health inducing features and benefits

Serves: 2

Calories: 696
Allergens:
Dairy

Crab Croquettes

Contributed by John Joyce

Ingredients

- 300g crab meat
- 200g breadcrumbs
- 100g flour
- 1 egg, beaten
- 3 tbsp olive oil

- 1 tbsp capers, chopped
- 2 tsp parsley, dried or fresh
- 1 sweet potato
- Salt & pepper
- 6-8 BBQ sticks/skewers

Method

1. Preheat the oven to 180°C.

2. Peel the sweet potato and cut into cubes. Add to a pan of water, bring to the boil and cook for around 5 mins. Check with a knife to see if the cubes are soft enough to mash with a fork, otherwise cook for a couple of mins more.

3. Add your crabmeat to a bowl with the capers and parsley. Give it a good mix up. When the sweet potato is ready, add this. Mash all together with a fork, then add around a tbsp of breadcrumbs. Mould the mix into small sausage shapes, insert a skewer and lay on a plate. When they are all shaped up, place into the fridge for 30 mins to firm up.

4. Remove from the fridge. Have 3 plates ready — one with the beaten egg, one with flour and one with the breadcrumbs.

5. Roll the croquettes in the flour, then egg and finally the breadcrumbs. Continue this with all the croquettes. In a large frying pan, add the oil and warm up over a medium heat.

6. Place 3-4 croquettes into the pan and allow them to colour up. You will have to roll them over gently so not to break them. When they are a golden colour, remove and lay on an oven proof tray. Once all are ready, place the tray into the warm oven to cook the croquettes through — 10 mins maximum should suffice. Check before you are ready to serve.

You could server these as party nibbles, or server with new potatoes and mint & cucumber riata!

Makes: 6-8

Calories: 244 per stick

Treacle Cured Salmon

Contributed by Jon Fell

Ingredients

- 1 side of salmon, skin on
- 80g treacle, slightly warm
- 1 tsp fennel seeds, crushed
- 1 lemon, zested
- 50g sea salt
- 1 tbsp English mustard
- 2 tsp cracked black pepper

Method

1. Place salmon skin side down on a tray that will fit into the fridge.

2. Cover tray with a sheet of greaseproof paper.

3. Mix all the ingredients together.

4. Pour the mix over the flesh of the salmon and coat well, massage in gently.

5. Cover with clingfilm and place into fridge.

6. Leave for three days to cure.

7. Remove from fridge, pat with kitchen paper to remove excess moisture.

8. Slice thinly and serve.

Serves: 6

Calories: 64
Allergens:
Seafood

Serve with a cream cheese and horseradish cream with brown bread, or, with a beetroot salad, or, just simply with a wedge of lemon

134

Sweet Chilli Prawns on Ciabatta

Contributed by John Joyce

Ingredients

- 1 ciabatta bread cut in half along the full length
- 225g king prawns
- 1 onion finely chopped
- 4 garlic cloves finely chopped
- ½-1 chilli chopped
- Bunch coriander
- Thumb size piece of ginger
- 5 tbsp sweet chilli sauce
- 1 tbsp olive oil

Method

1. Chop the onion, garlic, chilli, ginger, and coriander and put them in a tub with the prawns and chilli sauce and marinade for 10 mins.

2. Rub a little bit of olive oil and garlic over the top of the ciabatta.

3. Heat a large frying pan with the oil over a medium heat.

4. Now add the prawn and chilli mix to the pan, heat them through. This won't take long and a little shake of the pan will help to bring all the flavours together.

5. When they are ready remove and add across the top of the ciabatta.

6. Serve with a fresh salad.

Serves: 2

Calories: 428
Allergens:
Seafood

Cod on Stuffed Mushrooms

Contributed by John Joyce

Ingredients

- 2 cod fillets
- 2 tbsp olive oil
- 2 small cubes of butter
- Salt & pepper
- 2 large mushrooms

- 1 finely chopped small onion
- 2 large cloves garlic, crushed
- Any blue cheese you may have broken up
- Any dried herb of your choice

Method

1. Heat the oven to 200°C.

2. Clean your mushrooms up and add the finely chopped onion inside them.

3. Sprinkle some of your chosen herb over the top of the onions.

4. Finally add your blue cheese over the top of the mushrooms.

5. Place the mushrooms on a oven proof tray and place in the oven.

6. Season your cod fillets with salt and pepper across both sides.

7. Heat a frying pan over a medium heat and when hot add the oil and the fish.

8. Keep an eye on the mushrooms in the oven, if they appear to be turning brown to quick cover with foil.

9. After a couple of mins add the cubes of butter and tilt the pan to the side. Use a spoon to spoon over the melted butter and oil mix.

10. The cod will change colour again and it's easy to see how it cooks. I prefer cooking my fish on the top, for me you have more control over the finished fish meal.

11. The mushrooms should now be ready to remove from the oven.

12. Place the mushrooms on a plate and add the cod across the top of them. Serve with a fresh salad of sautéed potatoes. Again the choice is yours, use the oil/butter mix across the finished meal and enjoy.

Serves: 2

Calories: 360
Allergens:
Seafood

Pasta with Tomatoes, Olives & Tuna

Contributed by Nigel Edwards

Ingredients

- 8oz pasta (your choice)
- 1 small onion, diced
- 2 cloves garlic, crushed
- 1 tin chopped tomatoes
- 1 veggie stock cube
- ½ pint of boiling water
- 1 tin tuna in water
- Small jar of pitted black olives

Method

1. Put on pan of water, bring to the boil and add your pasta, cook until al dente.

2. In another pan sweat off the diced onion and crushed garlic in a little oil.

3. Once the onions have softened, add the tinned tomatoes and simmer.

4. Place stock cube in boiling water, mix and add to tomatoes.

5. Allow to simmer and reduce - if the sauce seems a bit thin, then add a tablespoon of tomato paste.

6. Drain the olives and slice.

7. Drain the tuna and flake.

8. Add the tuna and olives to the sauce and simmer for 2 mins, then add seasoning to taste.

9. The pasta should be done by now - drain off the water, and place in your serving dish or plate.

10. Place the sauce on the pasta, serve and enjoy.

Serves: 2

Calories: 429
Allergens:
Seafood

Chilli Mussels

Contributed by John Joyce

Ingredients

- 2 ripe tomatoes
- 2 tbsp olive oil
- 1 clove garlic, finely chopped
- 1 shallot, finely chopped
- 1 red or green chilli, deseeded and finely chopped
- Small glass dry white wine
- 1 tsp tomato puree
- Pinch of sugar
- 1kg cleaned mussels
- Handful coriander leaves

Method

1. Heat the oil in a large pan with a tight- fitting lid. Add the garlic, shallot and chilli, and then gently fry for 2-3 mins until softened. Pour in the wine and add the tomatoes, paste, sugar and seasoning (mussels are naturally salty so take care with the salt). Stir well and simmer for 2 mins.

2. Tip in the mussels and give them a stir. Cover tightly and steam for 3-4 mins, shaking the pan halfway through, until the shells have opened.

3. Discard any shells that remain shut, then divide the mussels between two bowls and add the coriander leaves. Provide a large bowl for the empty shells.

Serves: 2

Calories: 640
Allergens:
Seafood

Serve with garlic bread and enjoy

Fish on a Veg Bed

Contributed by John Joyce

Ingredients

- 1 salmon fillet for each person
- 1 head of fennel,
- 500g new potatoes cut in half and par boiled
- 2 red peppers chopped
- 3 red onions cut into thick slices
- 10-12 button mushrooms
- 6-8 large tomatoes cut in half
- 3 garlic cloves crushed
- 1 lemon cut into quarters
- 3-4 tbsp of olive oil
- Salt & pepper to taste
- Add any veg you wish or have to use up

Method

1. Heat oven to 180°C

2. Put all the veg into a roasting tin including the par boiled new potatoes. Now pour over the juice from 2 of the lemon quarters.

3. Add the olive oil. Season with salt and pepper and toss well.

4. Place the tray into the oven.

5. Every 10 mins or so remove the tray from the oven and give it another stir around.

6. After around 20 mins remove the tray and sit the fish on top of the veg and put in the oven until the fish is cooked.

7. As a rule of thumb, this should take around 10-15 mins.

Enjoy and serve perhaps with a crusty garlic bread

Serves: 2

Calories: 723
Allergens: Seafood

Cod Bites & Chips

Contributed by John Joyce

Ingredients

- 1 bottle sunflower oil, for deep-frying
- ½ teaspoon sea salt
- 1 tsp freshly ground black pepper
- 225g flour, plus extra for dusting
- 225g white fish fillets, use your local fishmonger
- 280ml beer, cold
- 3 heaped tsp baking powder
- 900g potatoes, peeled and sliced into chips

Method

1. Pour the sunflower oil into a deep pan heat it to 190°C.

2. Cut the cod fillets into bite size pieces.

3. Mix the salt and pepper together and season the fish fillets on both sides.

4. Whisk the flour, beer and baking powder together until nice and shiny. The texture should be like semi-whipped double cream.

5. Dust each cod bite in a little of the extra flour, then dip into the batter and allow any excess to drip off. Holding one end, lower the fish into the oil one by one, please be careful not to get splashed with the hot oil.

6. Don't overfill the pan with the cod bites, fry in batches if needed.

7. Cook for 4 mins or so, until the batter is golden and crisp.

8. Meanwhile, parboil your chips in salted boiling water for about 4-5 mins until softened and retaining their shape.

9. Then drain them in a colander and leave to steam completely dry.

10. To speed up the process dry them off with a little kitchen roll.

11. Now fry them off in the oil that the fish was cooked until golden and crisp.

12. While the chips are frying, place the fish on a baking tray and put them in the oven for a few mins at 180°C.

13. This will help them to stay crisp while you finish off the chips.

14. When they are done, drain them on kitchen paper, season with salt, and serve with the fish.

Enjoy with mushy peas and a slab of bread and butter

Serves: 2-3

Calories: 990
Allergens:
Seafood

Salmon topped with Filo Pastry

Contributed by John Joyce

Ingredients

- 3 tbsp olive oil
- 2 large shallots, finely chopped
- 140g chestnut mushrooms, finely chopped
- 3 garlic cloves, finely chopped
- Juice ½ lemon
- 100g packet watercress, chopped
- 2 tsp dill
- 1 tsp chive
- 6 sheets filo pastry each about 38 x 30cm (125g total weight)
- 2 skinned salmon fillets
- A little melted butter (around 2 small cubes)

Method

1. Heat 2 tbsp of the oil in a large non-stick frying pan. Tip in the shallots and fry for 2-3 mins to soften, and then add the mushrooms and garlic, and stir-fry over a high heat for another 3-4 mins, or until the mushrooms and shallots are golden and any liquid from the mushrooms has evaporated.

2. Pour in the lemon juice – after a few seconds, that should have evaporated too. Remove from the heat, then stir in the watercress so it wilts in the warmth from the pan, add the dill and chives, and season with a little salt and pepper. Leave to cool.

3. Preheat oven to 200°C.

4. Add your salmon fillets to an oven proof dish and place your sheets of filo onto a chopping board.

5. Cut the filo pastry into 1" strips, they can be smaller if you wish or wider. Now you will have filo ribbons to cover the salmon dish.

6. Cover the salmon with the mushroom mix and then lay out the filo ribbons over the top. Randomly cover the salmon and mushroom mix.

7. Lightly brush over the top of the filo with the melted butter, this will help to give it a golden colour.

8. Bake for 25 mins until the pastry is crisp and golden. Check while it cooks and if the top starts to brown too quickly, lay a sheet of foil very loosely over it.

9. Remove from the oven and let the salmon sit for 2-3 mins before slicing.

Enjoy with new potatoes or sautéed

Serves: 2

Calories: 317
Allergens:
Seafood

Seafood Paella with Chicken

Contributed by John Joyce

This meal has a bit of history in our home. In the early years of my cooking we held a party, during the evening as I was cooking. One of the guests asked me, "How many times have you cooked this"? I replied "We are going live tonight my good friend". Even then I had the confidence to have a go and it was simple to complete. Here's my way of doing it.

Serves: 6

Calories: 634
Allergens:
Seafood

Ingredients

- 2 chicken breast fillets or thighs chopped into nice pieces
- Sea salt
- Black pepper
- Plain flour, for dusting
- Olive oil
- Sliced chorizo, around 6-8 should be fine
- 1 onion, finely chopped
- 4 cloves garlic, finely chopped
- 2 ltr chicken stock, hot
- 2 large pinches saffron
- 1 heaped tsp smoked paprika
- 500g paella rice
- 2 tbsp dried parsley
- 4 tbsp frozen peas
- 1 lemon
- 1lb prawns, ask your fishmonger
- 500g mussels, ask your fishmonger

Method

1. Preheat the oven to 190°C.

2. Season the chicken pieces and dust with flour.

3. Heat a little olive oil in a large deep pan and fry the chicken until golden brown on both sides. Place the pieces on a baking tray and into the oven for 30 mins.

4. Put the pan back on the heat. Add the sliced chorizo and fry until browned and crispy.

5. Then add the onion and garlic and cook until soft.

6. Meanwhile infuse half the hot chicken stock with the saffron.

7. Add the, dried parsley, smoked paprika, rice and infused stock and leave to cook on a medium heat, stirring from time to time.

8. After 20 mins the rice should be nearly cooked.

9. At this point, pour in the rest of the stock along with the peas, prawns, and the mussels.

10. Place a lid on the pan and cook for 10 mins more.

11. Now add the cooked chicken.

12. Display all the paella nicely and serve with wedges of lemon.

Cod Fish Cakes

Contributed by John Joyce

Ingredients

- 450g cod fillets, ask your fishmonger
- 150ml milk
- 350g Maris Piper potatoes
- ½ tsp finely grated lemon zest
- 1 tbsp dried parsley
- 1 egg

- Flour, for shaping
- 85g fresh breadcrumbs, preferably a day or two old
- 3-4 tbsp veg or sunflower oil, for shallow frying
- 1 lemon cut into wedges
- 1 lemon juice and zest

Method

1. Lay the fish in a frying pan. Pour over the milk and 150ml water. Cover, bring to a boil, then lower the heat and simmer for 4 mins.

2. Take off the heat and let it stand, covered, for around 10 mins to gently finish cooking the fish.

3. Meanwhile, peel and chop the potatoes into even-sized chunks. Put them in a saucepan and just cover with boiling water. Add a pinch of salt, bring back to the boil and simmer for 10 mins or until tender, don't let them break up.

4. Lift the fish out of the milk with a slotted spoon and put on a plate to cool.

5. Drain the potatoes and leave for a couple of mins. Tip them back into the hot pan on the lowest heat you can and let them dry out for 1 min, mashing them with a fork and stirring so they don't stick. You should have a light, dry fluffy mash.

6. Take off the heat and beat in the lemon juice & zest, parsley and chives. Season well with salt and pepper. The potato should have a good flavour, so taste and adjust to suit.

Serves: 4

Calories: 491
Allergens: Seafood

7. Drain off liquid from the fish, grind some pepper over it, then flake it into big chunks into the pan of potatoes.

8. Using your hands, gently lift the fish and potatoes together so they just mix.

9. You'll only need a couple of turns, or the fish will break up too much.

10. Put to one side and cool.

11. Beat the egg on a large plate and lightly flour a board.

12. Spread the breadcrumbs on another plate.

13. Divide the fish cake mixture into four. On the floured plate and with floured hands, carefully shape into four cakes, about 2.5cm thick.

14. One by one, sit each cake in the egg, and brush over the top and sides so it is completely coated.

15. Sit the cakes on the crumbs, patting the crumbs on the sides and tops so they are lightly covered.

16. Transfer to a plate, cover and chill for 30 mins or even better the day before.

17. Heat the oil over a medium heat, in a large frying pan.

18. To test when the oil is ready, drop a piece of the dry breadcrumbs in - if it sizzles and quickly turns golden brown, it is ready to use.

19. Fry the fish cakes over a medium heat for about 5 mins on each side or until crisp and golden.

Serve with the lemon wedges for squeezing over and a fresh salad

Fish & Parsley Sauce

Contributed by John Joyce

Ingredients

- 1 cod or salmon fillet each person
- 3 tsp cornflour
- 300 ml milk
- 2 tbsp dried parsley
- 1 bay leaf
- 1 lemon, juiced
- Salt & pepper

Method

1. Place fish fillets in a saucepan, cover over with milk and a bay leaf and bring to the boil and simmer for about 15 mins. Lift the fish out with a slotted spoon gently when done.

2. Blend 3 tsp of cornflour with about 3-4 tsp of milk in a ramekin. Mix into a thick paste and add to a pan.

Add another dash of milk over a medium heat and whisk gently, keep adding the milk as you go. Keep whisking and adding more milk to you get the right consistency for you, add the dried parsley and whisk again. To give it an extra tang add the juice of a lemon and whisk again. Season with salt and pepper.

Serves: 2

Calories: 332
Allergens:
Seafood

Now serve your fish with new potatoes, sautéed or just on its own with the sauce poured over. Enjoy

Five Spice Salmon

Contributed by John Joyce

Ingredients

- 3 tbsp honey
- 4 tsp reduced-sodium soy sauce
- 1½ tsp five spice powder
- 2 large cloves garlic, crushed
- 4 (6 oz.) salmon fillets, pin bones removed
- 1 lb. slender green beans (haricot vert, if you can find them)
- 2 tsp olive oil
- 1 tsp sesame oil
- Salt & pepper
- 2 tbsp sesame seeds
- 1 tsp fresh lemon juice
- 2 small cubes of butter (to be added to the pan as the salmon cooks)

Method

1. In a small dish, whisk together the honey, soy sauce, five spice and garlic.

2. Put the salmon in a dish and pour the mixture over the top. Flip the salmon over so they are skin side up in the dish and let the salmon marinate for 15 mins or longer in the fridge.

3. Now heat a frying pan over a medium heat on the hob. Add the oil and place the salmon skin side down. Allow it to heat through, don't be tempted to move it too soon. You will notice the bottom of the fish changing colour and rising up as it cooks.

4. After a couple of mins you can add the cubes of butter and gently turn the salmon over just for a minute or so. Then turn it back skin side down and now slightly tilt the pan on its side. With a spoon, carefully spoon over the melted butter and oil across the top of the salmon. You will notice the turn a nice golden colour. Remove and serve with new potatoes or a fresh salad.

Serves: 4

Calories: 416
Allergens:
Seafood

Lamb & Beetroot Tagine

Contributed by Marcus Polakovs

Ingredients

- 6 pieces of round neck of lamb
- 2 onions, diced
- 3 cloves garlic, diced
- 3 carrots, 2 diced 1 sliced
- 3 sticks celery, 2 diced 1 sliced
- 1 tbsp tomato puree
- 3 whole beetroots, cooked and peeled
- 1 tin chopped tomatoes
- 1 pint chicken stock with a pinch of saffron
- Salt & pepper to taste

Method

1. Season lamb and fry in a stockpot with 1 onion and garlic, ensure lamb browned and onions translucent for 6-8 mins.

2. Transfer contents to a bowl and then add 1 onion, diced celery, diced carrot, to make a mirepoix by frying for 3-4 mins.

3. Meanwhile make the stock, add the puree.

4. Add the meat mixture back to the mirepoix, and add the stock mixture with saffron. Start layering.

5. Season well.

6. The sliced carrot and celery on top of the meat and mirepoix. Then add layer of tomatoes, then slice the beetroot and layer over the top.

7. Cook on the hob for 2-3 hours low heat.

8. Serve with new potatoes and crusty bread.

Serves: 6

Calories: 314
Allergens:
Celery

Lancashire Hot Pot

Contributed by John Joyce

Ingredients

- 100ml vegetable oil
- 300g lamb, cut into bite-sized chunks
- 1 tbsp tomato purée
- 1 tsp beef stock granules, dissolved in 100ml water
- 1 chopped onion
- 6 chopped carrots
- 2 sticks chopped celery
- Salt and pepper
- 6 medium potatoes sliced in about ¾ inch slices
- 2 tsp dried parsley, to garnish (optional)
- 100ml gravy, to serve

Method

1. Heat the oil in a heavy-bottomed pan/casserole dish. Add the lamb and cook until golden-brown and then stir in the tomato purée.

2. Add the stock and simmer for 2-3 hours, or until the lamb is tender.

3. Add the onion, carrots and celery and cook until the vegetables are soft.

4. Season to taste with salt and pepper.

5. Preheat the oven to 180°C.

6. Place the sliced potatoes on top.

7. Bake for 30 mins, or until the potato topping is golden-brown.

8. Sprinkle with dried parsley and serve with gravy.

This is a real winter warmer, enjoy!

Serves: 4

Calories: 632
Allergens:
Celery

Cordero Al Chilindron

Contributed by Keith Bradbury

Ingredients

- 1kg lamb shoulder or leg cut into even size chunks - I use leg mostly
- 5 cloves garlic, peeled and chopped
- Olive oil
- 100g serrano or parma ham – preferably cut in one thick slice then chopped
- 2 carrots peeled and sliced thinly
- 4 plum tomatoes quartered
- 1 red pepper, chopped
- Flat leaf parsley
- 100ml – maybe more – dry white wine
- 250g fresh peas – though tinned will be fine too

Method

1. Ok...pop the lamb chunks into a dish and mix well with the garlic – leave for up to an hour.

2. Heat a tbsp of oil in a sauté pan. Pan fry the ham for about 30 secs, then transfer to a casserole dish that has a tight fitting lid – you will be cooking on the hob, not in the oven. I use one of my stainless steel dutch ovens. Fry the lamb chunks next in same oil until browned, add to casserole. Sauté the carrots, then the peppers for about 5 mins each and add to the dish. Then the tomatoes until just starting to soften and colour. If need be add more oil at any point.

Serves: 4-6

Calories: 575

The idea is you want folk to be able to be served but not be shy about dipping into the main dish to get more juices!

3. Now add the wine and chopped parsley to the pan and let it bubble for a sec or two, then add to casserole with any scrapings.

4. Mix it all together. There should be about a couple of inches or so of wine – if not add a dash more and top up your glass at the same time – cook's perks!

5. Put on the lid adding a layer of foil first to make a really tight seal. Turn heat up high under the pot and cook on high for 20 mins – shake pan vigorously to stop it all sticking. Take a peep after maybe 15 mins and if necessary add a little more wine and turn heat down a little.

6. After 20 mins add the peas. Lid back on and cook for a further 20 mins. You can now, if you wish, just turn the heat off and move the pot to one side for 5 mins.

7. You will not believe that lamb can cook this fast and be so, so tender.

8. I serve on a white pre warmed dish to place in the centre of the table or in a pre warmed roasting tin, with shed loads of good crusty bread.

Contributed by Garmon Owen

Ingredients

- 1 neck of lamb cut in to slices. (You can ask your butcher to take off the bone but it adds more flavour left on the bone. If buying from supermarket just buy value lamb.
- 3-4 potatoes
- 1-2 carrots
- 1-2 parsnips
- Small swede or turnip
- 2 onions
- 1-2 leeks
- Salt & pepper
- Large 5 litre pan

Method

1. Coat the meat in some flour and brown both sides on a medium heat in the pan with a little oil.

2. Peel onions and the leeks and add to the pan.

3. You may need to add a little bit of water in to the pan to stop things from sticking.

4. Peel and chop potatoes, carrots, parsnips and swede and add to the pan.

5. Cover with water and add some salt and pepper to taste.

6. Bring to the boil, once boiling turn down heat so that it is just simmering.

7. Go and enjoy a beer and leave to cook for at least 2 hours.

Serves: 4-6

Calories: 376

Enjoy with fresh bread.
This dish tastes even better the second day warmed up or it can be frozen

Bacon & Pasta

Contributed by John Joyce

Ingredients

- 2 rashers streaky bacon
- 225g penne pasta
- 1 onion, chopped
- 1 clove garlic, finely chopped
- 340g grated Cheddar cheese
- 30g butter
- 3 tbsp plain flour
- 475ml milk

Method

1. Preheat oven to 180°C.

2. Place bacon in a large, deep frying pan. Cook over medium high heat until evenly brown. Drain, crumble and set aside.

3. In a large pot with boiling salted water, cook pasta until al dente. Drain.

4. In a medium frying pan, saute the chopped onion and garlic. Take off heat and add chopped cooked bacon and set aside.

5. To make the sauce, in a medium saucepan melt the butter over low heat. Once melted, add the flour and stir constantly for 2 mins. Gradually add milk and continue stirring until thickened. Stir in ⅔ of the grated Cheddar cheese and stir until melted.

6. Combine cooked pasta, sauteed vegetables and sauce. Pour into a 2 litre baking dish. Sprinkle over remaining Cheddar cheese.

7. Bake uncovered in preheated oven until cheese on top is melted and brown, 15-20 mins. Serve warm.

Serves: 3-4

Calories: 691

Sausage Casserole

Contributed by John Joyce

Ingredients

- 2 tbsp olive oil
- 1 onion, finely chopped
- 2 medium sticks celery, finely chopped
- 1 red pepper, chopped
- 3 cloves garlic crushed
- 3 chorizo sausages
- 6 pork sausages
- 2 tsp sweet smoked paprika
- ½ tsp ground cumin
- 1 tbsp dried thyme
- 125ml white wine
- 2 tins chopped tomatoes
- 2 sprigs fresh thyme
- 1 chicken stock cube
- 1 tin aduki beans

Method

1. Heat the olive oil in a large heavy-based pan/casserole dish. Add the onion and cook gently for 5 mins.

2. Add the celery and peppers and cook for a further 5 mins.

3. Add the sausages and fry the sausages for 5 mins, then stir in the garlic, spices and dried thyme.

4. Continue cooking for 1-2 mins or until the aromas are released.

5. Pour in the wine and use a wooden spoon to remove any residue stuck to the pan.

6. Add the tinned tomatoes, and fresh thyme and bring to a simmer.

7. Crumble in the stock cube and stir in.

8. Cook for 40-50 mins.

9. Stir in the beans and cook for a further 5 mins.

10. Remove the thyme sprigs.

11. Add salt & pepper to your taste.

Serves: 3-4

Calories: 451
Allergens: Celery

Serve with a nice roll to mop up the juices

156

Contributed by Sue Bush

Ingredients

- 450g-500g minced pork
- 2 medium carrots
- 1 large onion
- 2 small onions
- 2 medium eating apples
- 1 medium box Paxo stuffing
- 1-2 eggs

Method

1. Preheat the oven to 170°C.

2. Make stuffing according to packet instructions.

3. Grate carrots, onions and apple.

4. Mix with minced pork and made up stuffing mix.

5. Add one or two eggs to bind ingredients.

6. Place in a 2lb loaf tin and cook at 170°C for 1 hour.

Enjoy with your choice of sides

Serves: 4

Calories: 266

Leek & Bacon Risotto

Contributed by Phil Keenan

I love a nice, creamy risotto and, here, lovely fresh West Lancashire leeks and smoked bacon lardons combine to deliver a really tasty and comforting dish. Although a good risotto takes a little time at the hob stirring it, it's well worth the effort and is still a relatively quick dish to get to the table.

This is a really economical meal and works out at around £1 per portion

Ingredients

- 80g smoked bacon lardons
- 25g butter
- 1 medium onion - finely diced
- 2 large leeks - sliced
- 1 clove garlic - finely chopped
- 400ml Arborio rice
- 125ml white wine
- 1.5l chicken stock
- 50g parmesan cheese - finely grated
- 20g flat leaf parsley - chopped
- Salt & freshly ground black pepper

Serves: 4

Calories: 511
Allergens:
Dairy

Method

1. Have the stock, in a saucepan, keeping warm over a low heat.

2. Over a medium heat, gently fry the bacon lardons in a frying/ sauté pan until slightly golden.

3. Add the butter, leeks, onion and garlic, and fry until starting to soften but without colouring.

4. Add the rice and stir for a minute or two, until translucent.

5. Pour in the wine, stirring until absorbed.

6. Add the stock, a ladle at a time and repeat until the stock is used up or when the risotto is creamy in consistency and the rice just cooked.

7. Remove from the heat and stir through the parmesan and butter.

8. Season to taste and stir in the chopped parsley.

Casserole with Pork & Peppers

Contributed by Kirsten Huesch

Ingredients

- 300g pork (cubed)
- 1 tbsp vegetable oil
- 2-3 peppers (any colour)
- 1 large onion
- 1 clove garlic
- 2 tbsp tomato puree
- 1 vegetable stock cube
- 1 bay leaf

- Water
- Cornflour
- Optional: other seasoning such as chilli or paprika if you would like it to be a bit spicier or Italian herbs for a more Mediterranean feel

Method

1. Preheat the oven to 100°C (fan oven).

2. Dust the cubed pork with cornflour and set aside (Note: by using cornflour, the meat not only stays nice & moist but it also acts as thickener for the sauce).

3. Cut the peppers and onion into chunks; crush the garlic.

4. Heat the oil in an ovenproof pan on a medium heat and once hot, add the pork, vegetables, garlic and bay leaf.

5. Fry for 2 mins, then lower the heat and add enough water to just cover the ingredients.

6. Add the stock cube and stir in the tomato puree.

7. Transfer the dish to the oven and cook on a low temperature (100° in a fan oven) for at least 90 mins but longer if possible, checking now and again that there is enough liquid left in the pot - if not, add a little more water.

8. Adjust seasoning if required and serve with rice or mashed potato.

This dish also works very well with chicken or as a vegetarian alternative with lots of vegetables such as baby corn & mushrooms, reducing cooking time accordingly.

Serves: 3-4

Calories: 169

Chinese Pork Fillet & Noodles

Contributed by John Joyce

Ingredients

- 2 pork fillets
- 4 tbsp tomato ketchup
- 2 tbsp clear honey
- 2 tbsp soy sauce
- 2 tbsp sesame oil
- 1 tbsp five spice
- 2 cloves garlic, crushed

- 2 blocks egg noodles
- Any veg you wish to use to stir fry
- 2 tbsp olive oil
- 1 tbsp sesame oil
- 1-2 tbsp sesame seeds

Serves: 2

Calories: 839

Method

1. Put all the marinade ingredients into an oven proof dish and mix well.

2. Add the pork fillet and turn to cover in marinade.

3. Cover and chill for at least 2 hours or the night before in the fridge.

4. Preheat oven to 180°C. Prepare your veg.

5. Place the pork fillet and marinade into the oven and cook for around 30 mins.

6. Add the olive oil to the pan and stir fry your veg for 5-10 mins over a high heat.

7. Cook the noodles in boiling water.

8. Add a handful of sesame seeds to veg, then the sesame oil and fry for a further 1-2 mins.

9. When the pork is ready, remove from the oven and slice across on an angle.

10. Drain the noodles.

11. Now add the noodles to a plate, dress with the veg and sliced pork, drizzle over the remainder of the marinade and dress the plate up with the sesame seeds.

Hung Shao Pork

Contributed by Dave Davies

Ingredients

- 450g belly pork
- 4 tbsp dark soy sauce
- 25g ginger, minced
- 1 star anise
- 1 tsp ground cinnamon
- 1 tbsp caster sugar
- 3 tbsp rice wine or dry sherry

Method

1. Cut pork into one inch cubes and place in a heavy based frying pan skin down.

2. Sprinkle with soy sauce, cinnamon, star anise and ginger.

3. Add 1 tbsp of water bring to a boil and reduce heat to a simmer cover and cook on a low heat for 45 mins.

4. Turn over pork, then add caster sugar and rice wine or dry sherry. Recover and cook for another 45 mins on a low heat. Check now and again to make sure it's not dried out — add 1 tbsp of water if it is.

Serve with basmati rice.

Serves: 6-8

Calories: 444

Spiced Mandarin Orange Tea with Honey

Contributed by Croein Ruttle

Ingredients

- 4 tbsp honey
- 12 mandarin oranges - juice with the pulp
- 4 mandarin oranges - rind
- 4 cups water
- 4 star anise pods
- ½ tsp nutmeg, ground
- ½ tsp cinnamon, ground
- 1 cinnamon stick
- 1 tbsp vanilla extract
- Extra cinnamon sticks (optional garnish)

Method

1. Place all of the ingredients in a medium-sized saucepan. Cover with lid and heat over high heat. Stir every so often and bring to a boil. Turn the heat to low and boil for another 30 mins without lid, until all the flavours are well combined and the aroma of the spices is strong.

2. Before serving, strain the tea to remove the pieces of rind and any residue. Serve hot and decorate each cup with a stick of cinnamon if desired.

This is a wonderful winter warmer and can be sipped in front of a nice open fire

Serves: 6

Calories: 253

Lancashire Cheese & Onion Pie

Contributed by John Joyce

Ingredients

- 500g pack shortcrust pastry
- A drizzle of olive oil in the pan with around 20g of butter
- 3 onions (sliced thinly)
- 200g water
- Salt & pepper
- Around 250-300g of Lancashire Cheese, your own choice.
- 1 egg to seal the pastry and glaze the pie before it goes into the oven

Serves: 4-6

Calories: 599
Allergens:
Dairy

I like to make my own pastry but you can buy ready-made if you want to speed up the process

Method

1. Preheat your oven to 180°C.

2. Start by preparing your filling for the pie. Melt the butter in the pan with the olive oil on a medium heat. Add the sliced onions and slowly allow them to soften, aim to have soft onions and not scorched ones.

3. After around 10 mins add the water, salt & pepper to taste. Reduce the liquid by half and continue to gently stir the onions around the pan. Once ready, remove them from the pan and allow them to cool down on a plate.

4. I tend to grate the cheese now as the onions cool, grate the cheese into a bowl.

5. Lightly butter a loose bottom tin, or oven proof dish approx. 20cm wide and 5cm deep.

6. Take ⅔ of your pastry and roll it out to cover the bottom and sides of your chosen tin/dish. Your pastry needs to be around the depth of a one pound coin. Now carefully lay your pastry into the tin/dish.

7. Now add a layer of cheese in the bottom of the pie, then add a layer of onions and then a layer of cheese and repeat this process until you reach the top of the pie.

8. Make sure you fill the pie with plenty of the filling, once cooked and you cut into it you will want to see it full of filling.

9. Roll out the reminder of the pastry, crack your egg into a small dish and lightly brush the rim of the pie with the egg. Now lay the pastry lid on top of the pie, lightly press the edges of the pastry together and then trim the pie up. Add a couple of small holes in the lid of the pie, brush all over with the egg mix and bake in the oven for around 50 mins. I tend to keep an eye on mine from around 30 mins into the baking time, if you think the pie is becoming too brown cover with a piece of foil until its cooked.

10. The finished pie should have a golden colour and I allow it to cool down a little before serving. This is nice on its own or with mash potato and a splash of gravy.

Homemade Vegetable Quiche

Contributed by John Joyce

Ingredients

- 1 tbsp olive oil
- 1 pack shortcrust pastry
- 2 onions or 4 shallots - I used shallots as I had them
- ½ red pepper - this was leftover too
- 6-8 mushrooms, chopped
- 3-4 eggs
- 200ml milk
- 50-75g grated cheese- anything you have left
- 1 tbsp plain flour

Method

1. Preheat the oven to 180°C.

2. Spread some flour across the worktop and roll out the pastry to around £1 coin thickness to suit your ovenproof dish. Butter your dish and add the pastry. Fork the base of the pastry bottom. I blind bake my quiche case first.

3. Chop all the vegetables, add to a frying pan with a tbsp of oil and give them a gentle fry until all the vegetables have softened, then remove to one side.

4. Mix the eggs with the milk and a bit of the grated cheese.

5. Place the oven dish in the oven. I line the pastry with greaseproof paper and place baking beans on top but you can use uncooked rice instead. We want to blind bake the pastry - this should take no longer than 15 mins - you will see the pastry changing colour and firming up.

6. Remove from the oven, remove the baking beans and greaseproof paper and place the dish back in the oven - this time for 5 mins.

7. When ready, remove. Now let's make the quiche up!

8. Lay in your fried vegetable mix, pour your egg mixture on top and sprinkle over the remainder of the grated cheese.

9. Now bake in the centre of the oven for about 30 mins. If you think the top of the quiche is browning too quickly, cover with a piece of aluminium foil.

10. Remove when ready and allow to cool a little. I served mine with a fresh salad and salad dressing.

I just used vegetables and cheese from my fridge. Use your imagination and create great flavours

Serves: 8-10

Calories: 357
Allergens: Dairy

Chicken & Leek Pie

Contributed by Darren McDonald

Ingredients

- 4 large leeks, sliced
- Chicken (pulled from a roasted bird)
- 1 onion, finely chopped
- 2 bacon rashers
- 200ml double cream
- 1 ltr chicken stock
- 2 heaped tbsp plain flour
- 50ml olive oil
- 1 tbsp butter
- Salt & pepper
- 1 tsp English mustard powder
- A roll of puff pastry

Serves: 4

Calories: 513

Now it's your turn, go and make yourself look like a proper chef!!!

Method

1. Preheat the oven to 180°C.

2. This pie is best made using the stripped meat from a roasted chicken, we usually have lots of meat leftover after a Sunday roast. I've tried using chicken fillets chopped up and while it's okay, it just doesn't quite have that same wow factor. So I'm afraid you need to get your hands dirty with this recipe and get that lovely meat stripped off before you start cooking. Once you've finished stripping the meat off put it to one side while you prep the other ingredients.

3. Chop the bacon into small pieces and lightly fry with a glug of olive oil and butter until they start to brown. It is now time to add your onion and leeks.

4. Add both the leeks and onion to the pan, give it a good stir so that the oil and bacon gets thoroughly coated on the leeks. Turn the heat right down, grind in some salt and pepper, the mustard powder and put the lid on and let it simmer for about 30 mins stirring it occasionally.

5. It's at this point I like to add my two secret ingredients, a dash of Tabasco sauce to give it a little kick and a little garlic to shake it up a bit, but they aren't important if you prefer not to add them.

6. Your leek and onions should be nice and soft and the smell coming from them when you lift the lid is just another reason to cook this recipe!!! After the 30 mins simmering, add the chicken stock, the stripped off chicken meat, drop in the double cream and the flour and give it a stir. Season again with the salt and pepper, turn up the heat and bring to the boil stirring gently so as to avoid the mixture burning.

7. Place a sieve over a large jug and pour the contents of the pan into the sieve to allow the liquid to drain in to the jug. Congratulations, you've just made the basis for a gorgeous creamy gravy to accompany your pie, all you'll need to do is add some gravy granules prior to serving and re-heat...another smile factor for your guest/diners!!!

8. Transfer the now sieved contents of the pan to a deep sided pie dish/baking tin (35x25cm) and spread the mixture evenly in the tin. Time to lid the pie and as a famous person once said "life's too short to make pastry!" so to that end, open and roll out your shop bought puff pastry. Lay it on top of the dish, slice off the excess pastry and tuck the sides down so the mixture is covered. Egg-wash the pie and lightly score the pastry with a sharp knife. If you're feeling artistic, using the leftover pastry fashion into leaf shapes and place on top of the pie to add that little extra professionalism.

9. Place in the middle of the preheated oven for about 40 mins or until the pastry is nicely browned (not burnt). I like to serve to my guests with lovely creamy mash, some red cabbage and of course that delicious gravy.

Pork, Celery & Celeriac Pie

Contributed by Iain Devine

Ingredients

- 500g diced pork
- One peeled and diced celeriac, about the same in volume as the pork
- 1 head celery, peeled (this is important) and diced
- 1 large white onion, finely diced

- A large sprig of thyme
- Good chicken stock
- Double cream
- Mustard (optional)
- 200g beef suet
- 400g self-raising flour

Method

1. Fry the pork in a little oil in a large pan until browned - it's better to do this in smaller batches to get a good sear, remove to a colander over a bowl.

2. In the same pan gently fry the onion until soft but not coloured with the thyme.

3. Once soft & golden add the celeriac and celery and turn the heat up.

4. Keep stirring to stop the vegetables sticking.

5. Once softened (don't mind a bit of browning) add the pork back into the pan.

6. Turn the heat up to maximum and cover the ingredients with stock (it'll help if the stock is hot already).

I'm not going to give exact quantities here as you know how big your pie dish is and how many people you'll be feeding.

Serves: 4

Calories: 573
Allergens: Celery

7. Once it reaches a boil then turn the heat down to a simmer, leave to cook gently for 2-4 hours until the pork is tender.

8. Once the pork is done, fish out the thyme sprig - most of the leaves will have become detached - this is fine.

9. Turn the heat up and pour on double cream (and mustard if desired) and cook until the sauce has a nice thick consistency, season to taste.

10. Pour the filling into a pie dish. Preheat oven to 180°C.

11. You've got a choice of two things to hold the pie top up, 1) that ceramic black bird that's somewhere at the back of one of your kitchen drawers or 2) get your butcher to cut you a length on bone with the marrow in it, if you go for option 2 (and you should) make sure you serve the pie with chips to dip into the marrow.

12. Whichever you choose place in the middle of the pie dish and leave to cool, once room temperature put into the fridge

13. Meanwhile make the pastry, mix the flour & suet together, along with salt & pepper (and a touch of mustard powder if you like), splash on cold water and keep mixing until it becomes a smooth dough, you'll nearly always add too much water so it's a good idea to keep a bit of the flour/suet mix back to rectify this.

14. Flour a surface & rolling pin and roll out the dough to about 1.5 cm thick and top the pie, make a cross in the centre to accommodate the support, crimp the edges.

15. Any leftover dough can be rolled into balls and used as dumplings, or rolled thinner and used to decorate the top of the pie.

16. Brush the top of the pie with egg wash and place on a baking sheet into the oven.

17. The pie will be ready in 25-35 mins once the top has turned golden.

Honey Almond Biscotti

Contributed by Croein Ruttle

Ingredients

- ½ cup butter or margarine, softened
- ¾ cup local raw honey
- 2 eggs
- 1 tsp vanilla extract
- 3½ cups self raising flour
- 2 tsp anise seeds
- 2 tsp ground cinnamon
- ½ tsp baking powder
- ½ tsp salt
- ¼ tsp baking soda
- 1 cup dried cranberries
- ¾ cup slivered almonds

Method

1. Preheat oven to 220°C. Using electric mixer, beat butter until light; gradually add honey, eggs and vanilla, beating until smooth.

2. In small bowl, combine flour, anise seeds, cinnamon, baking powder, salt and baking soda; gradually add to honey mixture, mixing well. Stir in cranberries and almonds.

3. Shape dough into two 10x3x1" logs on greased baking sheet.

4. Bake for 20 mins or until light golden brown. Remove from oven to wire rack; cool 5 mins. Reduce oven to 180°C. Transfer logs to cutting board. Cut each log into ½" slices; arrange on baking sheet. Bake 20 mins or until crisp.

5. Cool on wire racks.

Makes: 40
Calories: 97
Allergens: Nuts

176

Syrup Sponge

Contributed by the pastry team
at George's Dining Room, Worsley

Ingredients

- 170g plain flour
- 1 tsp baking powder
- 170g soft butter
- 3 eggs
- 170g light brown sugar

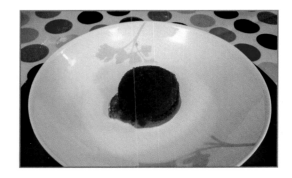

Method

1. Cream together the sugar and butter.

2. Add the eggs one at a time while mixing.

3. Pour in the flour and baking powder.

4. Use tin foil moulds and pour a blob of golden syrup in the bottom of them. This makes about 8.

5. Evenly distribute the mix between the moulds and bake in the oven at 160°C for 15 mins

We served ours still warm with double cream

Serves: 8

Calories: 335

Chocolate Ravioli with Mascarpone, Amaretti & Rum Stuffing served with Baileys Ice-Cream

Contributed by Mark Joyce

Ingredients

The Chocolate Pasta

- 125g/5oz strong/plain flour, sieved
- 50g/2oz cocoa powder
- 2 whole large eggs
- Pinch of salt
- 1 tsp caster sugar
- 1 tsp vegetable oil
- Extra flour to roll

The Mascarpone, Amaretti & Rum Stuffing

- 1 tbsp dark rum
- 8 crushed amaretti biscuits
- 2 tsp light brown sugar
- 1 small pot mascarpone cheese, approx. 250g
- 1 egg yolk

The Baileys Ice-Cream

- 300ml/10 fl oz milk
- 125g/5oz sugar
- 1 tsp vanilla extract
- 300ml/10 fl oz whipping cream
- 120ml/4 fl oz Baileys Irish cream liqueur

Serves: 8

Calories: 549

This was one of my dishes that was on my menu when I won my third AA Red Rosette. Test your culinary palette and let me know what you think!

178

Pre-Preparation – The Ice Cream

My personal tip would be to make this a day prior to serving.

1. Pour the milk, vanilla extract and sugar in a saucepan and gently cook over a medium heat, stirring until the sugar dissolves. Once the sugar has dissolved remove from the heat and cool.

2. In a large measuring jug, whip the cream until slightly thickened. Add the cooled milk mixture and whish thoroughly. Chill in the fridge for approximately 1 hour.

3. Add the Baileys, mix well and pour into an ice-cream maker. Freeze churn for 30-40 mins or according to the manufacturer's directions.

4. Alternatively turn the mixture into a rigid freezer proof container and freeze. Remove from the freezer every 20 mins; beat well with a wooden spoon until all ice particles have been broken up.

Method

5. First begin by preparing your mascarpone, amaretti and rum filling. Place the crushed amaretti biscuits in a small but deep container and spoon over the rum and sugar, leaving to soak.

6. In a small bowl mix the mascarpone cheese in with the egg yolk, whisk thoroughly and leave to one side.

7. For the pasta, begin by sieving the flour and cocoa together in a large bowl.

8. Once combined make a well in the middle of the bowl and drop in the eggs, oil, salt and sugar. Mix together well by hand until you form a consistent and sticky dough.

9. Knead with a little flour for 3-4 mins (see previous recipes on how to knead).

10. Cover the bowl with cling film and rest in the fridge for 20 mins or so.

11. Once the dough has chilled sufficiently work it through a pasta machine, at the highest setting, several times. Continue to do so though the next setting and so on until you eventually have a large, long rectangle.

12. Place on a floured worktop and cut into small/large rounds or squares – the choice is yours!

13. Place small spoonfuls of filling in the middle of one round/circle, egg wash the edges and place another round/circle on top.

14. Simply push down the sides to complete your ravioli and repeat stage 9 until all of the filling and pasta has been used.

15. Boil a large pan of water which contains salt and olive oil. When boiling point is reached cook the ravioli for 5-6 mins.

16. Drain off and serve immediately with your Baileys Ice-Cream or sweet alternative.

Yes it's true – you can make chocolate flavoured pasta. Simply fill it with an array of sweet fillings and serve with sauces like white chocolate cream, rum scented chocolate, Drambuie and orange milk chocolate sauce.

Eton Mess

Contributed by John Joyce

Ingredients

- 6 medium meringue nests
- 1 punnet strawberries (chopped into quarters)
- 1 jar of double cream (use as much or as little as you want)
- Ice cream (optional for decoration)

Method

1. Get your meringue nests and chop them into small chunks.

2. For you first layer put in a small amount of meringue in to the bottom of each dessert glass.

3. Chop up as many strawberries as you want for your Eton mess.

4. Place some strawberries on top of the meringue for your second layer.

5. Pour some cream over the top of the two layers but don't drown them in cream!

6. Repeat with the meringue/ strawberry/layer.

7. Now tip in the rest of the meringue into the glasses.

8. Pour more cream on top, as much as you want.

Decorate with chopped strawberries, a grating of chocolate the choice is yours.

Serves: 6

Calories: 530
Allergens: Egg

Egg Custard Tart

Contributed by David Skelton

Ingredients

Tart case

- 220g plain flour
- 150g butter unsalted
- 75g caster sugar
- Zest of 1 lemon
- 1 full egg and 1 egg yolk
  (free range if you can)

Custard filling

- 8 large egg yolks
  free range if you can
- 600ml double cream
- 80g caster sugar
- 5ml vanilla extract
- Nutmeg for grating

Serves: 8-10

Calories: 423
Allergens: Egg

Method

1. Rub flour and butter together until it looks like breadcrumbs, then stir in the lemon zest and sugar.

2. Now beat the egg and egg yolk in a separate dish. Once done add half the egg mixture to the flour and sugar mixing whilst you add (I use a knife to do this only because my Nana used to). If it needs more egg mixture, add a little more and keep mixing until it combines to a dough.

3. Once its ready use hands to make it into a dough ball and wrap in cling film and put in fridge for at least 1½ hours.

4. Preheat oven to 170°C.

5. Once the pastry has chilled roll it out on a floured surface until it's approximately 3mm thick (a pound coin thickness roughly). Now place this into a flan dish – the one I use is 9"/23cm. Don't worry about trimming perfectly around the edges at this time. That can be done later.

6. Now blind bake this for 12 mins. Once it's a nice golden colour remove the baking beans and parchment appear and brush the base of the case with egg yolk (this helps seal it whilst it cools off slightly).

7. Turn the oven down to 130°c.

8. Whilst oven is cooling place the 600ml cream in a pan over a medium heat and heat until it's a slow low boil (bubble around the edge) add the vanilla extract.

9. Whisk the egg yolks and sugar together.

10. Once cream has come to boil add a third to the egg mixture whisking all the time once it's mixed add the rest of the cream whisking thoroughly.

11. Now sieve the egg mixture and add to the pastry case and grate the nutmeg over it.

12. Bake in the preheated oven for approx. 30 mins until its firm to the touch but still has a nice wobble on it.

13. Allow to cool and serve as you like.

Chocolate Orange Tiramisu

Contributed by John Joyce

Ingredients

- 200g dark chocolate
- 50g butter, cubed/diced
- Sea salt
- 175g sponge fingers
- 400ml hot coffee (instant)
- 4 eggs

- 100g caster sugar
- 750g mascarpone
- 2 oranges
- ⅔ tbsp ground coffee

Topping

- 50g dark chocolate

Serves: 8

Calories: 560
Allergens: Egg

Pop into the fridge to firm up and enjoy!

Method

1. In a large dish add your instant coffee and add hot water. Lay in your sponge fingers. Make sure they all soak up the coffee mixture. If you can, turn them over and leave to cool.

2. Place a Pyrex or glass bowl over a pan of simmering water. Don't let the base of the bowl touch the water! Break up 200g of the dark chocolate & add to the bowl.

3. Now add the butter and a pinch of salt. Allow to melt — you can stir this gently to help it on its way. I add a squeeze of orange juice to this too.

4. Once the chocolate is melted and ready, pour over the sponge fingers and chill.

5. Now it's time for the eggs. Separate the yolks and whites into bowls, ready to whisk.

6. Add the sugar to the yolks and whisk on a high setting with an electric whisk or - if you want to release some stress — by hand. Continue until all the sugar has dissolved, then mix in the mascarpone and the zest of one orange.

7. Wash your whisk, dry and then whisk the whites with a pinch of salt until they form soft peaks.

8. Now add your whites to your yolk mix and gently fold them together.

9. Right, let's finish the tiramisu off! Lay the creamed mixture on top of the sponge fingers. Smooth it evenly across the dish. Using a potato peeler peel the 50g of the chocolate over the top of the dish. Get as arty as you wish here — make it a crowd pleaser for the table!

10. Sprinkle over with grated orange zest — again make sure you cover the whole top with the zingy orange.

Bread Pudding

Contributed by David Pratt

Ingredients

- 8oz stale bread
- 6oz dried fruit
- 3oz suet or lard
- 2oz sugar
- 3oz flour
- 2 level tsp mixed spice
- 1 egg
- A little milk

Method

1. Preheat the oven to 150-160°C.

2. In a bowl soak the bread in a little water for about ¼-½ hour, then remove the bread and squeeze the water out.

3. Mix the flour with the suet or lard, then add the sugar, mixed spice, fruit and the soaked bread.

4. Beat the egg with a little milk and stir into the bread mix, making a soft mixture.

5. Pour into an ovenproof dish and bake in the oven on the middle shelf for 1¼ hours.

Serves: 6

Calories: 326
Allergens: Egg, gluten, clove

Malteser Mousse

Contributed by David Skelton

Ingredients

- 4 egg whites
- 70g sugar
- Pinch salt

- 100g dark chocolate, broken into squares
- 2 x 37g packets Maltesers (holding back a few for the top)

Method

1. Melt the chocolate and crushed Maltesers in a large heat-proof bowl over simmering water (making sure that the base of the bowl doesn't touch the water) until it has completely melted. Set aside to cool.

2. Meanwhile, whisk the egg whites, sugar and salt in a large mixing bowl until stiff peaks have formed. Use an electric whisk - it's easier! Beat about a ⅓ of the egg whites into the cool chocolate mix. You don't have to be delicate here: it's just a case of introducing the egg whites to the chocolate roughly.

3. Next, delicately fold the second ⅓ of the egg whites into the bubbly chocolate mixture until well mixed and it gets lighter.

4. Finally, when all the white air pockets have gone, fold in the remaining third of egg whites into the chocolate mixture and repeat the delicate folding in technique until the mixture is a uniform texture and colour.

5. Place in small pots and leave to chill in fridge.

6. When serving crush the few Maltesers you have left and sprinkle over the top.

Serves: 6

Calories: 204
Allergens: Egg

 Lemon Meringue Cheesecake

Contributed by Debbie Halls-Evans, Home Of Real Food

Ingredients

- 100-150g digestive biscuits
- 50-75g butter — melted
- 100g lemon curd (or make your own)
- 320g cream cheese
- 2 fresh lemons, juiced & zested
- 1 lime (optional 1 x juice & zest)
- 75g icing sugar (sieved)
- 4 egg whites (weigh them)
- Caster sugar (double the weight of the egg whites)

Equipment

- Pie/Cake tin or small mini muffin tin
- Rolling pin
- Plastic bag (freezer bag) or Tea Towel
- Whisk or electric blender/food processor
- Oven
- Piping bag (optional)

Personalisation

- Change the base to any of your favourite biscuits, ginger nuts, chocolate chip, rich tea, or a shortbreads for rich base most biscuits work

- For a richer Lemon cream use a mix of Ricotta 80-100g, Mascarpone 80-100g and Cream Cheese 160g

Serves: 8

Calories: 350
Allergens: Egg

You can add flavouring to your meringue, lemon zest for an extra lemony kick

Method

1. Bash the biscuits up in the bag or between a tea towel, or in your food processor until breadcrumb texture, add to melted butter.

2. Put the combined biscuit mixture into your cake tin, or mini muffin tin, push down to create a base.

3. Add a layer of lemon curd and chill base and lemon curd in fridge while you make the rest of the cake.

4. Whisk the cream cheese with icing sugar, lemon juice and lemon zest tighter until very smooth – put aside and chill.

5. Put the caster sugar in the oven on 100°C and allow to warm, whisk the egg whites until soft peaks, remove the sugar and pour into whisked egg whites and whisk for another 5-8 mins until thick peaks and glossy.

6. Now layer the cake, on top of the base, lemon curd, add a thick layer of the lemon cheese cream, and either pipe the meringue into peaks or pile up on top of your cheese cake- you can use either a cooks torch or pop under the grill for 5 mins to brown.

7. Chill for 15 mins and serve. Grate some extra zest over the top when serving.

Lemon Curd recipe:

- 4 medium eggs, plus extra yolk, 4 lemons (juiced and zested), 150g butter, 250 grams sugar.

- Melt the butter in the microwave or in a pan. Whisk eggs, sugar, juice & zest. Add butter and keep stirring until thickens. Jar and keeps for about 4 weeks, Or use for recipe.

- You can change the cream topping to just using limes and then use chocolate cookies for the base.

- Use almond cookies for the base and add chocolate to your cream cheese mix without the lemons for a rich nutty chocolate meringue add chopped nuts.

189

Lemon Crunch Layer Cake

Contributed by Helen McDonald

Ingredients

Cake:

- 250g soft butter
- 300g white sugar (caster or granulated, doesn't really matter)
- 4 large eggs
- 300g self-raising flour
- 2 tbsp lemon curd

Crunch topping

- 4 tbsp granulated sugar
- 2 tbsp lemon juice

Filling:

- 80g butter
- 20g lemon curd
- 250g icing sugar

Method

1. Preheat the oven to 180°C.

2. Grease and line 2x 20cm loose bottomed tins (if you don't use loose bottomed ones it's just slightly more fiddly to remove the cakes... I don't have loose bottomed tins!).

3. Cream the butter and sugar together until light and fluffy. This can be done either by hand with a wooden spoon or a hand held whisk/food mixer.

4. Add the eggs one by one, beating well.

5. Add the flour and fold in, followed by the lemon curd.

6. Spoon the mixture into the 2 tins and level the tops with the spoon/spatula.

7. Put into the oven on the middle shelf and bake for 30 mins or until a skewer comes out clean.

8. The cakes will look darker than a normal sponge due to the lemon curd.

9. For the topping; mix the granulated sugar and lemon juice together and spoon over the top cake while it is still hot. Leave to cool in the tin.

10. For the filling; mix the butter and lemon curd together then add the icing sugar gradually. The result should be a fairly firm buttercream. Add more icing sugar if desired, some people like a firmer buttercream.

11. Once the cakes have cooled, remove from the tins and spread the filling on the top of one of the cakes and sandwich the two together.

Slice and serve...with pouring cream if you are feeling extremely naughty?!

Serves: 8-10

Calories: 612
Allergens:
Egg, dairy

White Chocolate & Berry Muffins

Contributed by Rebecca Chester

Ingredients

- 55g butter
- 125g plain flour
- 125g caster sugar
- 1 egg
- 4 tbsp milk
- 1 tsp baking powder
- Pinch salt
- 100g blueberries/raspberries
- 75g white chocolate chips

Topping

- 130g icing sugar
- 100g cream cheese
- 70g butter
- 2 tbsp blueberry/raspberry jam

To decorate

- 50g blueberries/raspberries
- 25g white chocolate chips

Makes: 6

Calories: 581
Allergens:
Egg, dairy

Method

1. Line a muffin tin with 6 large cupcake or muffin cases.

2. Preheat the oven to 180°C.

3. Sieve the baking powder, flour and salt together in a bowl.

4. Rinse and pat dry the blueberries/raspberries with a paper towel, place in a bowl with the chocolate chips and sprinkle on a dessert spoon of flour to coat them both.

5. Cream the sugar and butter together until light and fluffy. Start with a wooden spoon and finish using an electric hand mixer if you have one.

6. Add the egg and mix well using the electric mixer.

7. Beat in the flour and milk a few spoonfuls at a time.

8. Stir in the blueberries/ raspberries and white chocolate chips using a cutting/folding motion.

9. Share the mixture amongst your cases, they should be around ⅔ full.

10. Bake for 25-30mins until golden brown and firm but springy to the touch. Remove and allow to cool.

Method for topping

11. Combine the icing sugar butter and cream cheese with a wooden spoon, then beat well with an electric mixer until smooth.

12. Spoon in the jam, cut through the mixture a couple of times but don't stir it in.

13. Once the muffins are cooled spoon the topping mixture into a piping bag or a plastic bag and snip the end or one corner, pipe in swirls on top of the muffins.

14. Finish with the fresh blueberries/ raspberries and a few chocolate chips.

Pancake Tower

Contributed by John Joyce

Ingredients

- 50g sugar
- 100g flour (plain or self raising)
- 1 egg
- Splash of milk

Method

1. Add the flour and sugar to a bowl.

2. Add egg and mix into flour/sugar using a whisk.

3. You will now have a dry lumpy mix you want to smooth this out by gradually adding splashes of milk until it resembles double cream.

4. In a dry hot frying pan add a ladle of batter.

5. Once it starts to bubble flip it over.

6. Cook for 2 mins and then remove from the pan.

7. I kept mine warm in a warm oven in foil until ready to build the tower. Use any ice cream/fruit/chocolate sauce. The choice is yours.

Serves: 1

Calories: 594
Allergens:
Egg, dairy

Bread and Butter Pudding

Contributed by David Pratt

Ingredients

- 8 slices bread, buttered
- 2oz dried fruit
- 2oz sugar
- ½ pint milk
- 1 egg

Method

1. Preheat the oven to 180°C.

2. Cut the buttered bread into small squares.

3. Put half the dried fruit into a buttered ovenproof dish and top with half the sugar.

4. Top with half the bread squares, then repeat the same for another layer.

5. Beat the egg with the milk and pour the mixture over the bread.

6. Place the dish into the middle of the oven and bake for approx. 20 mins.

Serves: 3-4

Calories: 204
Allergens: Egg

Lemon & Orange Polenta Cake

Contributed by John Joyce

Ingredients

- 200g soft unsalted butter (plus some for greasing)
- 200g caster sugar
- 200g ground almonds
- 100g fine polenta
- 3 large eggs
- Zest of 2 lemons (save the juice for syrup)
- Zest of 2 oranges (save the juice for the syrup)

Serves: 8-10

Calories: 409
Allergens:
Egg, dairy

Enjoy this cake on its own or even with cream.

Method

1. Line the base of a 23cm/9inch spring form cake tin with baking parchment and grease its sides lightly with butter.

2. Preheat the oven to 180°C.

3. Beat the butter and sugar till pale and whipped, either by hand in a bowl with a wooden spoon, or using a freestanding mixer.

4. Mix together the almonds, polenta, and beat some of this into the butter-sugar mixture, followed by 1 egg, then alternate dry ingredients and eggs, beating all the while.

5. Finally, beat in the lemon/orange zest and pour, spoon or scrape the mixture into your prepared tin and bake in the oven for around 40 mins.

6. You may think it's a bit wobbly but, if the cake is cooked, a cake tester should come out clean and the edges of the cake will have begun to shrink away from the sides of the tin.

7. Remove from the oven to a wire cooling rack, but leave in its tin.

8. Make the syrup by boiling together the lemon and orange juice and icing sugar in a smallish saucepan.

9. Once the icing sugar is dissolved into the juice, it's ready.

10. Prick the top of the cake all over with a cake tester (a skewer would be too destructive), pour the warm syrup over the cake, and leave to cool before taking it out of its tin.

Spiced, Iced & Sliced Lime + Ginger Cake

Contributed by Sue Currie (Netherton Foundry)

Ingredients

- 125g butter
- 100g golden syrup
- 50g black treacle
- 2 eggs
- 2 limes
- 125g self raising flour
- 1½ tsp ground ginger
- ½ tsp mixed spice
- 100g icing sugar

Method

1. Preheat the oven to 170°C

2. Cream the butter with the syrup and treacle.

3. Beat in the eggs.

4. Pare the rind of one lime and reserve for decoration.

5. Add the finely grated zest of the other lime and the juice of 1½ limes and mix thoroughly.

6. Fold in the flour and spices.

7. Line a 1lb loaf tin with a butter paper of baking parchment.

8. Spoon the mixture into the loaf tin and level the top.

9. Bake for 30 mins.

10. Allow to cool in the tin for 10 mins, then turn out onto a rack, remove the paper and allow to cool.

11. Make the icing by mixing the icing sugar with the remaining lime juice, adding a little water if necessary.

12. Spread the icing over the cake, cut the reserved lime peel into thin strips and scatter over the top.

Serves: 16

Calories: 147
Allergens:
Egg, dairy

Simple Green Vanilla Panna Cotta

Contributed by Michael Dundon

Ingredients

- 3 gelatine leaves
- 250ml/9fl oz milk
- 250ml/9fl oz double cream
- 25g/1oz sugar
- 1 pear
- 1 vanilla pod, split lengthways, seeds scraped out or vanilla extract will do
- Green tasteless food colouring

Method

1. Soak the gelatine leaves in a little cold water until soft.

2. Place the milk, cream, vanilla pod and seeds or extract and sugar into a pan and bring to a simmer. Remove the vanilla pod and discard.

3. Squeeze the water out of the gelatine leaves, then add to the pan and take off the heat. Stir until the gelatine has dissolved then stir in a few drops of food colouring until you get the desired colour.

4. Divide the mixture among four ramekins and leave to cool. Place into the fridge for at least an hour, until set.

5. Chop the pears into small squares and place in water to keep their colour.

6. To serve turn each panna cotta out onto a serving plate (sit the ramekin in hot water for a minute this will make turning out easy) and arrange chopped pears around the panna cotta.

This is a very easy to do and tasty dessert.

Serves: 4

Calories: 372
Allergens: Dairy

Cherry Loaf

Contributed by Sue Currie (Netherton Foundry)

Ingredients

- 125g butter
- 125g sugar
- 2 eggs, at room temperature
- 50g ground almonds
- 75g self raising flour
- 100g dried cherries
- 2 tsp grated lemon rind (optional)

Method

1. Preheat the oven to 170°C.

2. Cream the butter and sugar until light and fluffy.

3. Add the eggs and lemon rind and beat again.

4. Fold in the flour, almonds and cherries.

5. Line a 1lb loaf tin with butter papers, greaseproof paper or a loaf liner.

6. Transfer the cake mixture to the tin, level the surface and place in the oven.

7. Bake for approximately 25 mins. Please remember that ovens vary, so it's worth keeping an eye on your cake the first time you bake it.

8. Check that the cake is cooked through — insert a skewer into the centre of the cake and if it comes out clean your cake is cooked.

9. If the cake is not cooked through, but the top is golden, cover with a loose sheet of greaseproof paper or foil, I use a butter paper, to prevent the top from burning, while the middle cooks.

Serves: 8-10

Calories: 217
Allergens:
Egg, dairy

200

Caramel Banana Pudding

Contributed by Sue Currie (Netherton Foundry)

Ingredients

- 400ml milk
- 150g sugar
- 3 eggs
- 2 bananas, mashed
- 125g breadcrumbs

Method

1. Preheat the oven to 180°C and butter a casserole dish.

2. Put 100g of the sugar into a pan our saucepans are ideal for this.

3. Heat gently until it turns golden brown. Do not be tempted to stir it, just watch closely!!

4. Carefully pour in the milk - you may want to cover your hand with a cloth, as it can spit.

5. Stir well to mix and make sure that all of the caramel dissolves into the milk.

6. Beat eggs with remainder of the sugar.

7. Heat the caramel milk to near boiling and pour over the egg mix. Whisk.

8. Mash the bananas to a smooth pulp.

9. Put bananas and breadcrumbs in a mixing bowl and pour over the egg and milk mixture.

10. Mix thoroughly.

11. Pour the mixture into the casserole dish and put into the oven.

12. Cook for 20 mins, until just set.

13. Remove from the oven and leave to stand for 10 mins before serving.

Serves: 4

Calories: 415
Allergens:
Egg, dairy

201

Aunt Janice's Lemon Cake

Contributed by Nigel Edwards

Ingredients

- 4oz soft margarine
- 6oz self-raising flour
- 2 eggs
- 1 tsp baking powder
- 6oz caster sugar
- Zest from 1 large lemon
- 4 tbsp milk

Method

1. Preheat the oven to 180°C, put all the ingredients into a mixing bowl and mix until smooth.

2. Pour the mixture into a greased 8" tin.

3. Bake for 50-60 mins.

4. Take the juice from the large lemon and mix it with 4oz of caster sugar.

5. When the cake is cooked, place on a cooling wire and pour over the lemon/sugar mix.

Serves: 8-10

Calories: 230
Allergens:
Egg, dairy

When the cake has cooled, cut the cake, sit back, relax and enjoy

Chocolate Brownies

Contributed by the pastry team
at George's Dining Room, Worsley

Ingredients

- 175g chocolate
- 175g unsalted butter
- 3 medium eggs
- 250g caster sugar
- 75g plain flour

Method

1. Preheat the oven to 150°C.

2. Melt the chocolate and butter over a Bain-Marie.

3. In a bowl mix the sugar and eggs gently.

4. When the chocolate and butter have melted mix in with the sugar and eggs.

5. Mix in the flour.

6. Pour the mixture into a oven dish lined with grease proof paper and bake for 35 mins.

7. Let it cool a bit and enjoy it slightly warm.

Serve with ice cream or single cream while still warm for a perfect winter pud!

Serves: 9

Calories: 399
Allergens:
Egg, dairy

Fruit & Seeds Flapjack

Contributed by Kirsten & Martyn Burnett

Ingredients

- 250g salted butter
- 125g soft brown sugar
- 5 tbsp of golden syrup
- 100g jumbo rolled oats
- 300g porridge oats
- 60g large raisins
- 60g dried cranberries
- 40g pumpkin seeds
- 40g sunflower seeds

Utensils

- Your largest saucepan
- 20 x 20 x 5cm deep - square silicone baking tin
- Tablespoon
- Weighing scales

Serves: 16

Calories: 289
Allergens: Dairy

We like to call this "healthy" flapjack but it's not really,... it is really tasty though!

Method

1. Preheat the oven to 180°C.

2. Lightly butter the baking tin.

3. Over a low heat melt the butter in the saucepan.

4. When all the butter has melted add the sugar and the syrup. I use squeezy syrup for ease and I coat the tablespoon in butter so that the syrup doesn't stick too much. Mix until the sugar has melted.

5. Add the jumbo oats, all the dried fruit and seeds and mix well. (I use jumbo and porridge oats to create a better texture, if you only have porridge oats this is fine but don't use only jumbo oats as the mixture doesn't bind well enough).

6. Finally add all the porridge oats and mix well.

7. Put the mixture into the tin and press it down with the back of a spoon.

8. Bake for 25 mins or until golden brown.

9. Remove from the oven and leave to cool. When using a silicone baking tin it isn't advisable to cut the flapjack in the tin, so cool in the fridge and then press the whole block out onto a board where it can be cut, with a sharp knife, into whatever size you choose. I generally cut the block into 3 equal oblongs and then cut each oblong into 6 fingers.

Stored in an air tight container in the fridge, they will easily last for a week. They also freeze brilliantly.

Try warming 2 or 3 flapjacks up in the microwave for 20 secs and serving with a scoop of ice cream to use as a dessert or just eat them as a snack from the fridge.

These were tested on fussy kids, so are suitable for use in lunchboxes or as a quick breakfast snack for those lazy bones!

Shortbread

Contributed by the pastry team at George's Dining Room, Worsley

Ingredients

- 900g plain flour
- 800g unsalted butter
- 300g caster sugar
- 300g cornflour
- 3g salt

Method

1. Preheat the oven to 140°C.

2. Melt the butter in a pan.

3. Mix all the ingredients together in a large mixing bowl.

4. Put the mix onto a greased baking tray and use a rolling pin to roll it evenly to about 2cm thick.

5. Prick gently with a fork all over and lightly cover with caster sugar.

6. Bake at 140°C for 40 mins.

7. Portion it into rectangular biscuits while still slightly warm and leave to cool before eating.

Makes: 32

Calories: 351
Allergens: Dairy

We baked a quarter of the recipe into a shallow baking tin to form triangles - perfect for those afternoon tea moments with friends!

Flapjacks

Contributed by John Joyce

Ingredients

- 175g butter
- 175g soft brown sugar
- 1 tbsp golden syrup
- 250g porridge oats

Method

1. Preheat oven to 150°C. Lightly grease a 20cm baking tin.

2. In a large pan, melt together the butter, sugar & syrup, while stirring.

3. When melted, remove from the heat and stir in the porridge oats.

4. Pour into tin and smooth the surface with a spoon. Bake for 35-40 mins or until the edges are brown and the surface has turned golden.

5. Place the tin on a wire rack. Cut into squares after 10 mins, but leave to cool completely before removing from the tin.

6. You can add various fruit of your choice to make them different.

I have tried various recipes for these over the years, this one works every time and this for me is the best.

Serves: 16

Calories: 183
Allergens: Dairy

White Chocolate & Cranberry Blondies

Contributed by John Joyce

Ingredients

- 225g caster sugar
- 4 eggs
- 225g butter, melted, plus extra for greasing
- 150g sifted plain flour
- 225g chopped white chocolate
- 100g dried cranberries

Method

1. Preheat the oven to 180°C.

2. Grease a 8 inch square cake tin.

3. In a bowl, beat together the sugar and eggs until pale and fluffy. Beat in the melted butter a little at a time, making sure each addition of butter is fully mixed before you add anymore.

4. Add the flour and carefully fold this into the mixture using a metal spoon.

5. Add chopped white chocolate and cranberries and carefully fold this into the mixture.

6. Now spoon the brownie batter into the prepared cake tin and shake gently until level.

7. Place in the oven and bake for 30-35 mins, or until a skewer inserted into the centre of the brownie comes out clean.

8. Remove and allow to cool, enjoy as a sweet treat.

Serves: 16

Calories: 281
Allergens:
Eggs, dairy

Lemon Posset

Contributed by Sue Bush

Ingredients

- 500ml light creme fraiche
- 5oz caster sugar
- Juice of 2½ lemons

Method

1. Heat creme fraiche and sugar on a low heat, stirring occassionally.

2. When simmering reduce heat and add juice of lemons.

3. Simmer gently for 2 mins.

4. Pour in to ramekins and chill for 8 hours.

Top with meringue for the ultimate dinner party dessert! Great for cleansing palettes while being scrummy enough to eat on its own as a naughty treat!

Serves: 3-4

Calories: 251
Allergens: Dairy

Fruit Scones

Contributed by John Joyce

Ingredients

- 250g plain white flour
- 2 tsp baking powder
- 45g golden caster sugar
- 40g butter cubed (unsalted)
- 100g sultanas
- 1 egg
- 75ml milk

Method

1. Preheat the oven to 220°C and line an oven proof tray with baking parchment.

2. Sieve the flour and baking powder into a large bowl and add the sugar and butter, rub together until the mixture resembles breadcrumbs then add the sultanas.

3. In a jug beat together the egg and milk then pour into the bowl and mix using a round bladed knife until a dough forms, then knead a little with lightly floured hands until smooth. Add a little more milk if the dough seems to dry.

4. Bring the dough together and lay out on a lightly floured surface to a thickness of about 3-4cm, then using a 5cm round cutter cut 8 scones.

5. Place these on the baking tray, leaving about 5cm space in between, brush the tops with a little milk then bake in the oven for 15-20 mins until they are golden brown and the scones have risen.

Remove and cool on a wire rack, then cut them in half, serve with jam and clotted cream.

Serves: 8

Calories: 195
Allergens:
Egg, dairy

210

Rum Truffle Cake Balls

Contributed by John Joyce

Ingredients

- 250g leftover cake (loaf cake, sponge, pound cake - nothing creamy though)
- 2 tbsp rum (you can leave this out & double the rum flavouring instead)
- 2 tbsp rum flavouring
- 60ml hot water
- 30g icing sugar
- 2 tsp cocoa powder
- 25g coconut oil, melted (optional - these will also stick together without the addition of the extra fat)
- Chocolate sprinkles for decoration
- Paper muffin cases

Method

1. Crumble the cake into a bowl.

2. Mix the hot water, rum and rum flavouring and pour over the cake crumbs. Mix to distribute evenly and leave to soak in for a little while. The flavour will continue to develop, so don't be tempted to add more rum at this stage.

3. Melt the coconut oil (if using), leave to cool slightly and then mix together with the icing sugar and cocoa powder into the cake crumbs.

4. Stir everything and form the mix into 8 balls (approx. 50g each). Roll in chocolate sprinkles, place in a paper muffin case and leave to rest in the fridge for a couple of hours.

Remove from the fridge an hour before serving to allow to get to room temperature.

Serves: 8

Calories: 166

211

Blackpool's Young Carer Quotes

The quotes below are just a few from the recent #cookerysos lessons where I have been showing them how Simple fresh food can be cooked.

When asked to describe the session in 3 words, answers included: *Perfect, Fun, Great, Skillful, Good Exciting, Learning, Spending time with friends*.

"I have enjoyed working as a group and meeting new people. I have had fun for the last 4 weeks and I have learnt how to make different things. I thought it would be like school but it was completely different and I have really had fun."

"It was a new experience that I liked and I will use these skills in the future".

"Cooking was extremely fun and all of the people were very nice, I think many carers would benefit from this and I look forward to using these skills in the future".

"I have learnt a lot of things about cutting and cooking food, the best bits were just chilling and talking".

When asked what their favourite part of the session was answers included:

"Eating the food we cooked and meeting new people. It was lovely".

"Cooking with everyone".

Our Sponsors

This book would not have been possible without the kind donations and support of our sponsors. Please join us in thanking them for their time, donations and support.

Popular Conversion Tables

Oven temperatures

Most of the recipes in this book (unless otherwise stated) are set for conventional ovens. Where you are using a fan assisted oven, we suggest you reduce the temperature by 20 degrees (although individual oven performance may vary).

We recommend the use of an oven thermometer and/or meat thermometer to help you double check.

Oven Temperature		
Gas Mark	°F	°C
1	275	140
2	300	150
3	325	170
4	350	180
5	375	190
6	400	200
7	425	220
8	450	230
9	475	240